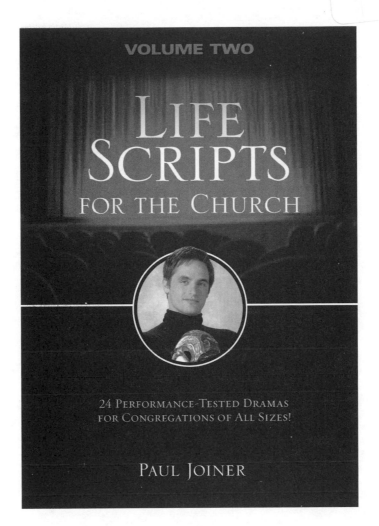

VOLUME TWO

LIFE SCRIPTS

FOR THE CHURCH

24 PERFORMANCE-TESTED DRAMAS
for CONGREGATIONS OF ALL SIZES!

PAUL JOINER

NELSON REFERENCE & ELECTRONIC

A Division of Thomas Nelson Publishers

Since 1798

www.thomasnelson.com

LIFE
SCRIPTS
FOR THE CHURCH

Volume 1

Volume II

Characters

Holiday

More than 400 individual scripts available online
for purchase and download

www.thomasnelson.com/drama

VOLUME TWO

LIFE
SCRIPTS
FOR THE CHURCH

24 PERFORMANCE-TESTED DRAMAS
FOR CONGREGATIONS OF ALL SIZES!

PAUL JOINER

Published in Nashville, Tennessee, by Thomas Nelson, Inc.

Nelson books may be purchased in bulk for educational, business,
fundraising, or sales promotion use. For information, please email
SpecialMarkets@ThomasNelson.com.

Nelson books may also be purchased in bulk for ministry use by churches,
parachurch ministries, and media ministries. For information, please call
(800) 251-4000 ext. 2804 or email NelsonMinistryServices@thomasnelson.com.

All Scripture quotations, unless otherwise noted, are taken from the
King James Version of the Bible.

Managing Editor W. Mark Whitlock
Edited by Steffany Woolsey
Book packaging by Design Point, Inc.
Interior Design by Bennett Davis Group

Library of Congress Cataloging-in-Publication Data available upon request.

Printed in the United States of America

ISBN: 141850985X

06 07 08 09 10 11 12 RRD 9 8 7 6 5 4 3 2 1

A Word
About Copyrights

Wait a minute. Wait! Stop the show. Hold the curtain. Don't cue the lights.
Hold everything.

The side-splitting and soul-touching scripts you hold in your hand were
written for you. Paul Joiner and Thomas Nelson can't wait to see
God use you and drama in your local church.

We want you to win.

We've built the copyright rules to help you put on these productions
with the least amount of struggle.

DO make copies of the scripts for your actors, technical crew,
and pastoral staff.

DON'T keep them. After the production is complete, please destroy them.

DO tell your peers about the success you're having with drama.

DON'T lend those copies or your book to other churches. If they want
to see samples, please send them to www.thomasnelson.com/drama
for more information.

DO include the dramas on any recordings you make of your services.

DON'T sell copies of the performances only. It's fine to include the presentation
of a script in the context of your worship service. However, when you
sell copies of your presentation of a script by itself or with other dramas,
you're breaking the copyright. You'll need to secure permission from us
before you do so. Send your request on church letterhead to:
Nelson Reference, P.O. Box 141000, Nashville, TN 37214.

DON'T forget to put credits on the recordings. Here's a sample sentence
for you. "The dramatic presentation, 'Heavenly Hash,' is used by permission
of the author and Thomas Nelson, Inc. ©2006 Paul Joiner."

DO tell us about how God is using the dramas in your life.
Go to www.thomasnelson.com, click on "contact us," and send us an email.

May God richly bless you . . . and your audiences.
May your productions point to the Cross.

Sincerely,

The Publisher

TABLE OF CONTENTS

SEARCHING FOR A GREAT SCRIPT

Fifteen years ago I launched a new drama ministry in our church. It was far from an instant success. In fact, our early performances were met with a fair share of boos, hisses, snores, and the occasional well-targeted tomato (all delivered in Christian love, of course).

A big part of the problem was that back then, the only dramas I could find were either too long, too "churchy," too difficult to produce, too predictable, or too boring.

Something had to change. Any stage fright I had ever known was nothing compared to this new and paralyzing phobia: *script fright*.

Thus began my search for the right script.

. . . .

SCENE: **Mountain Top**

(PAUL JOINER stands at the top of a mountain, screaming out to the cruel and unimaginative world below . . .)

Paul: Is there anyone out there who has written church dramas that are fresh, creative, and can minister to my church?

(PAUL's words echo throughout the cavernous land below. No response comes. All we hear is the screech of a vulture, a distant thunderclap, and a church member picking up another tomato.)

(PAUL desperately tries again . . .)

Please, can anyone help me find good—no, good and *effective*—church drama? I am sick of mediocre scripts! I can't seem to find what I am looking for . . . I am willing to travel to the ends of the earth just to find the right script!

(Once again PAUL's words echo through the land. Then the wind suddenly stops blowing. The earth's creatures go silent. And just as Paul is hit with a juicy red tomato . . . he hears a voice from the valley below.)

Voice: If you don't like what's out here, then get off that mountain, get down here with the rest of us, and write your own stuff! It ain't that easy, pal!

(So PAUL wipes tomato seeds from his brow, climbs down off his mountain, and gets busy writing scripts. And he soon finds that the VOICE was right: "It ain't that easy.")

. . . .

After fifteen years of writing scripts, here's what I've learned: Great church drama *always* begins with a great script. You can have the best actors, technical support, props, and costumes in all the land, but if your script doesn't deliver a *LIFE* situation in a creative, imaginative, and timely manner . . . well, let's just say it's curtains on your drama ministry.

So what should you look for in a quality church drama script? The following ten criteria are crucial to the success of your drama ministry.

A Truly Great Script . . .

1   Complements the theme of the sermon or event.

Why are you looking for a script? Is its purpose to introduce the pastor's message? Is it to promote a church campaign? Perhaps the role of your drama is simply to provide quality entertainment, or to celebrate a special event or holiday.

Whatever the purpose, your script should be relevant and meaningful to the occasion. Take a broad subject and narrow it to a particular focus. It might help to ask your pastor or worship leader this simple question: "What thought or lesson do you want our congregation to leave with after this service?" The answer to this question is the "thesis statement" of your drama.

Now match a script to that focus. Don't be afraid to adapt a script to make it fit perfectly with what you are trying to achieve.

2   Introduces the pastor's sermon—but <u>never</u> preaches it for him.

A good script introduces and illustrates the focus of the message to come. Whether the script has a resolved or unresolved ending, be sure that it leaves your audience wanting to hear and learn more. When you produce good introductive dramas, you'll find that it prepares the hearts of the congregation for the pastor's message.

I've found that the most effective way to prepare a congregation's hearts for the message to come is through one of three responses: laughter, tears, or wonderment.

3   Sets the mood for the sermon.

Wow, did I ever learn this lesson the hard way! There is nothing worse than having a hilariously funny drama precede a serious sermon topic like death and mortality. On the other hand, nothing introduces a sobering sermon message like tithing better than a comedic spoof.

Be aware of how your pastor wants the hearts of the congregation prepared before the sermon. Find a script that is light and funny when you need to "lighten the mood." If you want to ready the audience for a profound topic, choose a script with a more serious tone.

After a few emotionally misguided dramas, you'll discover why it is so important to know where the drama is scheduled in the service, what precedes and follows it, and how the pastor wants the congregation to receive the Word.

4   Takes no more than five or six minutes to perform.

Let's face it: Most church dramas are *too long*. You should be able to get your point across in six minutes or less. Short, sweet slices of life are infinitely more effective than long, drawn-out mini-productions.

Just remember that the attention span of the people in the pews is very short. So capture their attention by illustrating your point or introducing a new idea in a fresh way. The key is to leave them wanting more—and a good script will do just that.

5   Has interesting characters and plotline.

Unique characters and a well-conceived plotline will guarantee a well-received drama. A good plot should be unveiled slowly—don't give it away all at once. And a good script should have solid character development to help your congregation relate to whatever situation is playing out onstage.

6 Calls for three or more characters.

I've found that with a cast of three or more actors, the memorization load is considerably lightened—and the dynamic of the presentation much more interesting. I generally feel that a drama with four to five actors is better for the actors *and* audience than the heavy commitment required for a one- or two-character sketch.

7 Is performed easily on your church's platform.

Look for scripts that can be easily adapted to your facility. A good sketch should work within your allotted stage area as well as your church's lighting and sound capabilities. If a script calls for trap doors, smoke, flash pots, intensive lighting, or a complicated set and props list, you may just want to avoid it.

Also, a good sketch will be a one-scene presentation—a simple, concise slice of life. Multiple scenes that require multiple stages, lighting cues, scenery, and costume changes get way too complicated for church dramas.

8 Is never too advanced for your actors' abilities.

Know beforehand the abilities, experience, and commitment level of your actors. Choose a script that will stretch your actors without frustrating or defeating them.

Ask yourself, *Can my drama team pull this off?* Read through the script and determine how much memorization, rehearsal time, and energy will be required. You always want to grow your actors with challenging material, but remember that a good church drama program should slowly develop the skill of its actors— one drama at a time.

9 Possesses the Four C's.

A good script contains four important elements:

- *Clever* approach to a familiar subject

- *Concise* beginning, middle, and end

- *Clear-cut* message (stated or understated)

- *Connection* to the audience: emotional, physical and/or spiritual

You'll discover that dramas containing all Four C's will be well-received by your pastor, actors, and congregation.

10 Appeals immediately to the director (you)!

How do you know when you have a great script in your hand? When you can't *wait* to perform it.

When you read through a great script, you immediately begin to envision what it will look like performed. You'll laugh out loud. You'll tear up. You can't wait for your church to experience the plot, characters, and message of the script you are reading.

A good script will change people, helping them see things just a little differently than before. And you can't wait to share it!

Like I said, I believe the material in all four volumes of *Life Scripts* meets each of my criteria for a good script. You're holding twenty-four scripts in your hands now . . . and there are just as many in every other edition.

So what are you waiting for? Jump in and make the dialogue and characters on these pages come to life. They've been tried and tested, and are easy to perform.

Lights! Camera! Ministry!

HIS understudy,

Paul Joiner

MR. & MRS. LUCKY

with Cecil & Penelope

TOPIC
Thanksgiving: being thankful

SYNOPSIS
John and Patricia Clemens catch a quick lunch break together and discuss their upcoming Thanksgiving plans. It doesn't take too long to see that John and Pat are complainers, prone to focusing more on what they *aren't* thankful for than on what they actually have. Cecil and Penelope, a local street couple who are somewhat learning/mentally disabled, appear on the scene. Cecil and Penelope's contentment in poverty teach John and Pat a valuable lesson about thankfulness.

SETS/PROPS
Sketch should take place at a sidewalk cafe or in the park with Patricia and John sitting on a park bench. Cecil and Penelope should have a couple of trash bags full of "stuff" they have collected from the streets.
Patricia and John both need to-go deli sandwiches and sodas in paper cups.

CHARACTERS

John – Middle-aged, husband to Patricia

Patricia – Middle-aged, wife to John

Cecil – Homeless, mentally disabled man

Penelope – Homeless, mentally disabled woman

NOTE: Penelope and Cecil's mental condition should not be overdone to the point of being distracting or offensive. Their mental disability should make them charming, sincere, and innocent, not comical.

LIGHTS:	**BLACKOUT** (*Actors move into place*)
SOUND:	**TRANSITION INTO SKETCH**

(PATRICIA and JOHN sit at a bench, opening carry-out deli sandwich bags)

John: This was a great idea, Pat. Meeting for lunch is about the only time we can talk without the kids or other distractions.

Pat: And we need to talk about our Thanksgiving plans for tomorrow.

John: Right. What kind of sandwich are we splitting?

Pat: Turkey.

John: Turkey? Pat . . . in just a few hours we are going to have turkey coming out our ears. Why did you order us a turkey sandwich?

Pat: Honey, I'm sorry. I wasn't thinking.

John: I don't want to eat it. I won't be in the mood for turkey tomorrow.

Pat: Then let's talk about tomorrow. You are aware that *all* the family will be there, yours and mine?

John: Aunts and uncles, too?

Pat: Aunts, uncles, nephews, nieces . . . I think even a few dogs-in-law are coming too.

John: Who's footing the bill for the Thanksgiving dinner?

Pat: I'll give you three guesses.

John: Us, again? We are going to need a prehistoric-size turkey to feed all of them. What's it going to cost us?

Pat: John, we are the only ones in the family with a six-figure income.

John: Good thing . . . 'cause we get to feed half the city this Thanksgiving.

Pat:. Sorry. I know things have been difficult for us lately.

John: That's an understatement. Our new house isn't going to be completed on time. Our trip to Europe is being postponed. We've been fighting the flu! What's next, Pat?

Pat: I don't know. With all of our troubles, it makes it tough to imagine sitting around the table tomorrow giving thanks.

SOUND: **CECIL AND PENELOPE'S ENTRANCE**

(PENELOPE and CECIL enter. They look around and cross to another bench not too far from JOHN and PAT. JOHN and PAT look a little uncomfortable as the odd-looking couple draws nearer. JOHN and PAT continue . . .)

▸ *Drama Cue: Meet Cecil and Penelope*

Cecil and Penelope are endearing characters, and should be portrayed as such— sweet, childlike characters who have moments of silliness. No baby talk here, just simple-minded adults who view God as their Father and visitors to the park as new friends.

Pat:	Anyway . . . even though we aren't in the mood for tomorrow's celebration, at least . . .
Cecil:	Hello, Happy Thanksgiving!
Penelope:	Happy Thanksgiving!
	(PAT and JOHN are caught off-guard)
Pat:	*(Apprehensively)* Hello . . .
Penelope:	You're a very lovely couple.
Cecil:	You're very lucky, very lucky.
John:	*(Still apprehensive)* Thank you . . .
Cecil:	Are you celebrating Thanksgiving tomorrow?
John:	Yes, we are.
Penelope:	Very good.
Cecil:	I bet you are celebrating with friends and loved ones. Am I right?
Pat:	Yes we are.
Cecil:	You're so lucky.
Penelope:	That sounds like a wonderful time.
Cecil:	I bet you're going to eat a big fat turkey too.
John:	Yes, very big, and very fat.
Cecil:	You're so lucky. You're very lucky.
Penelope:	Very good.
Pat:	*(Being polite)* And where will you two be for Thanksgiving?
Cecil:	Depends how far we get today. Probably spend it on Fifty-fourth Street, under the bridge.
	(PAT and JOHN look at each other and realize the state of the two they have encountered.)
Pat:	Will you be spending the day with family?
Penelope:	We don't got any family. It's just us.
Cecil:	Our families sort of disappeared. Penelope doesn't know her real family . . .
Penelope:	Cecil's took him to a special camp and didn't come back to get him.
Cecil:	Oops! I'm not very lucky, huh?
John:	Hmm. You live out here?

▶ *Caution:*
Character Actors

When choosing actors for character roles, cast people whose physical stature and features don't interfere with their transforming into someone "different." You'll find that some actors can become anything you want them to be, while others will always be "themselves." This is the difference between straight actors and character actors.

Cecil:	Yep. I bet you live in a house, right?
John:	Uh-huh.
Cecil:	You're so lucky.
Penelope:	You've got a pretty car too, huh?
Pat:	*(Looking at her husband as if to make sure he understands the situation that's unfolding)* Yes, two very nice cars.
Cecil:	You're so lucky. Happy Thanksgiving!
Pat:	Thank you . . . happy Thanksgiving to you.
John:	It's nice to meet both of you, but we've got to be getting back to work.
Cecil:	You've got a job?
John:	Yes.
Cecil:	You're so lucky. What's your name?
John:	My name? I'm John Clemens.
Cecil:	No you're not. You're Mr. Lucky . . . that's who you are! Mr. Lucky!
Penelope:	And you're Mrs. Lucky!
	(PAT and JOHN are taken aback for a second)
Cecil:	Happy Thanksgiving, Mr. and Mrs. Lucky!
John:	You like Thanksgiving?
Penelope:	Very much so.
John:	Why? You have nothing. What do you have to be thankful for?
SOUND:	?
	(PENELOPE and CECIL look at each other)
Cecil:	*(Slowly looking back to John)* We're alive, aren't we?
Penelope:	We have each other.
	(Silence as all four share the moment)
John:	Happy Thanksgiving Cecil, Penelope.
	(CECIL and PENELOPE watch PAT and JOHN walk away. Then PAT returns and hands them the bag containing the sandwich.)
Cecil:	Thank you.
	(PAT and JOHN exit)
Penelope:	Food? What did we get?

Cecil:	Let's see.
	(PENELOPE and CECIL sit down and open the bag. PENELOPE takes out the turkey sandwich and holds it up . . .)
Penelope:	Look Cecil, our Thanksgiving turkey!
Cecil:	You know who we are? We're Mr. and Mrs. Lucky!
	(PENELOPE places the turkey and wrapper on the bench. She and CECIL fold their hands, bow their heads, and begin to pantomime giving thanks for their Thanksgiving dinner.)
LIGHTS:	**FADE TO BLACK**
	END

OVERPOWERED

TOPIC

Bible: The power of God's Word in our lives.

SYNOPSIS

A stolen briefcase brings a street thug to the Lord, all because
of the power of God's Word.

CAST

David

Jack

Kayla

SET/PROPS

Sketch takes place in a downtown alley of a large city. Props needed
are a briefcase with a lock, a Bible, and a wad of money.

LIGHTS:	BLACKOUT *(Actors move into place)*
SOUND:	MUSIC TRANSITION INTO SKETCH
GRAPHIC:	TITLE SLIDE— *Overpowered!*
LIGHTS:	UP ON STAGE

(It's nighttime in a back alley of a downtown metropolitan city. DAVID enters the alley. DAVID is well groomed, yet has an edge to him. He stops and looks around. After a few moments a figure appears behind him in the shadows.)

Jack: *(Spoken from the shadows)* David? David Henderson?

(DAVID begins to turn around)

Don't turn around. You're fine right where you are.

David: *(Looking straight forward)* I'm David Henderson.

Jack: Are you alone?

David: Yes. You?

Jack: No, so don't try anything.

David: I won't . . . just take it easy.

(JACK emerges from the shadows and crosses to DAVID. His right hand is inside his jacket.)

Jack: You should know I've got a gun.

David: You also have my briefcase.

Jack: First things first. You got my money?

David: Yes.

Jack: You look familiar to me. You a cop?

David: *(Sighs)* No. Do I look like a cop?

Jack: You don't look like no business executive.

David: I'm not one of those either.

Jack: Then why a briefcase?

David: I don't have a briefcase. Remember? Some street thug overpowered me on the city bus and stole it!

Jack: Yeah, well, you need to be more careful where you put your briefcase. The tag had your name and phone number on it.

David: Lucky for you, or you couldn't hold my briefcase for ransom. *(Reaching into his pocket)* Now, how much do you want?

Jack: Hey, easy! Keep your hands where I can see them.

▸ *Drama Cue:*
Minimal Lighting

Lighting, or lack thereof, can really set a mood. To present a feeling of imminent danger or peril, use less lighting. A dark stage filled with shadows cast across the set can really create a mysterious atmosphere.

David:	All right! Relax.
Jack:	*(Nervously)* Don't tell me to relax! Man, I know I've seen you before!
David:	Am I going to get my briefcase or not?
Jack:	Okay! Okay! I'm running the show here! Shut up and just do what I say!
	(DAVID puts his hands out, palms forward, as if to say, "Fine, whatever.")
	Where's the money?
David:	In my right pocket.
	(JACK pats down DAVID's front pocket.)
Jack:	All right, go slow.
	(DAVID reaches into his pocket and pulls out a wad of bills.)
David:	You said seventy-five, right?
Jack:	One hundred! I want one hundred bucks now!
David:	Okay.
Jack:	One hundred and twenty! And . . . and a percentage of whatever is inside!
David:	Hey, slow down.
Jack:	There must be something pretty special inside that briefcase for you to pay this much for it!
David:	You mean you didn't open it?
Jack:	You had it locked.
David:	You could have broken it open.
Jack:	You guys pay more when your stuff isn't messed up!
David:	Okay, a hundred and twenty bucks . . . and . . . I will share whatever is inside with you. Deal?
Jack:	*(Reaching for the money)* Deal.
David:	*(Pulling the money back)* First let me see the briefcase.
Jack:	*(Calling toward the shadows)* Kayla!
	(KAYLA emerges from the shadows carrying DAVID's briefcase. She looks just as nervous as JACK.)
Kayla:	Jack, what's taking so long? Where's the money?
Jack:	I'm working on it!

▶ *Caution: Key Light*

When employing a shadow-lit stage, be sure that there is one designated light illuminating the actors' faces clearly. This is known as a key light— a light that illuminates the front of the action.

Kayla:	Is this him?
David:	So you're Kayla, and this is Jack. You know, it's probably not a good idea to use each other's names when you're robbing someone.
Jack:	*(To Kayla)* I've told you that before!
Kayla:	You said my name too, Jack!
Jack:	Kayla!
David:	Can I have my briefcase?
	(JACK and DAVID nervously exchange the briefcase and the money. After the exchange, JACK quickly counts the money and DAVID looks his briefcase over.)
Jack:	A hundred and twenty. *(Gives the money to Kayla)* Here. Go.
Kayla:	Aren't you coming?
Jack:	I'll be right behind you after I get a little bit of what's inside the case! Now go!
Kayla:	Bye, Jack. Oops!
Jack:	Kayla, go!
	(KAYLA exits with the money. JACK turns back to DAVID)
	Now unlock the briefcase and let's get this over with.
David:	Do I really have to share what's inside with you?
Jack:	Yes! Hurry it up!
David:	All right.
SOUND:	**BRIEFCASE INTERACTION BACKGROUND**
	(DAVID quickly enters the combination into the briefcase's lock, then slowly opens the briefcase. All that is inside is a large Bible. JACK sees the Bible, grabs the briefcase, and shakes it upside down.)
Jack:	A Bible? That's it? That's all that was inside this whole time?
David:	That's right.
Jack:	That's not worth a hundred and twenty bucks!
David:	I could buy a cheaper Bible, but this Bible has special meaning. You see, this is the Bible that changed my life. This is the Bible that gave me the power to change who I was.
Jack:	What are you talking about?
David:	So you really don't recognize who I am?
Jack:	*(Trying to remember)* I keep thinking I know you, but . . .

David:	Davey? D? That's what everyone called me when I dealt drugs out here in the streets.
Jack:	*(Slowly recognizing him)* D. It is you. You look so different. You've gained some weight . . . cut your hair . . . cleaned up. You were the baddest . . .
David:	I know. You don't have to say it.
Jack:	So how did you do it? How did you get clean?
David:	*(Holds up the Bible)* This. It's amazing what power God's Word can have in your life. I'm clean. Have a job. And I'm studying to be a minister.
Jack:	You, a minister? Unbelievable. Wow, D . . . I'm glad for you. Hopefully someday I'll get out of the mess I'm in. See you later.
	(JACK begins to leave.)
David:	Hey.
	(JACK stops and turns around)
	I thought we had a deal? I was supposed to share what I had in the briefcase with you. You got a minute?
Jack:	I'm afraid I'm too far gone for that to do any good.
David:	I don't know. This Book is pretty powerful.
Jack:	*(Softening)* But what about the money you paid me?
David:	*(Indicating the Bible)* This is worth the ransom. Hey, let me tell you about Someone who paid a ransom for you.
Jack:	Me?
David:	Yeah. Let me show you.
	MUSIC SWELLS
	(DAVID and JACK sit down on some boxes in the alley. DAVID opens the Bible and begins to share the scriptures with JACK.)
LIGHTS:	**FADE TO BLACK**
	END

The Control Panel

TOPIC
Holy Spirit: being controlled by the Holy Spirit.

SYNOPSIS
Joe's emotional Control Panel is meeting for an emergency session. Each panel member represents a controlling emotion in Joe's life: Fear, Anger, the Flesh, and Worry. Up until now, Joe has put the control of his life in the hands of the Control Panel. But now Joe has become a Christian, and there will be a new member on the panel: the Holy Spirit.

SETS/PROPS
The Control Panel should be sitting at a table covered with a black tablecloth, with each panel member's name displayed before them. A remote control device is needed, and Control Panel members should have notes and files spread out in front of them as if they're at a planning meeting. A large calendar should hang behind the panel, with "JOE" written at the top of it and dates, etc., scribbled on the days. (A desk calendar can be used for this.)

CHARACTERS

Fear – Mafia type

Anger – tough guy

Flesh – movie celebrity

Worry – executive nerd

LIGHTS:	BLACKOUT *(Actors move into place)*
SOUND:	MUSIC TRANSITION INTO SKETCH
GRAPHIC:	TITLE SLIDE— *The Control Panel*
LIGHTS:	UP ON STAGE

(FEAR, ANGER, FLESH, and WORRY are standing around the panel table, engaged in a heated discussion. They are all talking at once, and each is trying to take possession of the remote control device. WORRY and FLESH are sitting on the upstage side of the table, and ANGER and FEAR sit on either ends of the table. Finally, WORRY speaks . . .)

Worry: Gentlemen! Gentlemen, please! Stop it! We're getting nowhere.

Anger: *(Pointing to FEAR)* You've been in control for a full three days! Now it's my turn!

Flesh: Yeah, let someone else have a chance!

Fear: If you think you're tough enough to take the controls out of my hand, go for it!

Anger: You don't want to make me mad!

Worry: If we don't quit fighting like this, Joe's going to have a nervous breakdown . . . or an ulcer! What then?

Fear: Okay! I'm dropping the controls in the middle of the table and no one's going to touch them until we check the master calendar. Fair?

(Everyone agrees)

Worry: Thank goodness! Gentlemen, Joe has been kind enough to let us control his life. Whether it be *(points as he goes)* Fear, Worry, the Flesh, or Anger, we each get our turn. Now, as members of Joe's emotional Control Panel, I say we stick to the calendar.

Anger: I agree with you, Worry! So what's Joe got going on today?

Worry: *(Looking at the calendar)* Well, according to Joe's schedule, we are just about to go into a meeting with Joe's boss!

Anger: Man, I hate that guy!

Flesh: Anger's right. He isn't paying Joe what he's worth.

Worry: Fear?

Fear: Joe's been afraid long enough. Maybe a little anger would be good for him.

Worry: I guess it is unanimous, Anger, you're in control!

(ANGER picks up the remote control, examines it, points the remote upward/outward, and with an exaggerated motion pushes the button on the remote)

▸ *Drama Cue:*
Representatives

When characters represent emotional or spiritual qualities, accent their portrayal through hairstyle, makeup, wardrobe, and speech patterns. For example, if a character represents Worry, the actor should dress conservatively, keep actions close to his body, and fidget throughout the presentation. Anger might be made up to look like a member of a gang or the Mafia.

Anger:	Done! He's mine!
Flesh:	For a while. But tonight, I'm in control!
Worry:	How's that, Flesh?
Flesh:	It's the weekend. I've got big plans for Joe!
Fear:	Then he's mine come Monday morning!
Worry:	Sorry, I'm on Monday morning with regret.
Anger:	My turn when his wife asks questions!
Worry:	Okay, listen. Up until now, we have pretty much fought over the controls of Joe's life. Every man for himself. Right?

(Guys acknowledge)

Well, I have some bad news. We are getting a new Control Panel member. *(Men react)* And if you or I want any chance of being in control, we are going to have to work together instead of against each other.

Flesh:	Someone new in control? Who is it, Pride?
Worry:	No, not him.
Anger:	So . . . who's the new guy?
Worry:	The Holy Spirit.

(Panel reacts with shock)

Fear:	How did this happen?
Worry:	Remember the other day when Flesh was supposed to keep Joe away from church? *(To FLESH)* Well, you didn't do a very good job . . . and Joe became a Christian!
Anger:	Why, I oughtta punch you out!
Flesh:	Yeah, right. Your bark is bigger than your bite!
Fear:	*(Pointing at FLESH)* You're gonna pay!
Flesh:	Joe may be afraid of your threats, but I'm not!
Worry:	Please, gentlemen! We need to work together!
Anger:	You're right! So what's Joe going to do now, just hand over the controls to the Holy Spirit?
Flesh:	The Holy Spirit isn't even around, is He?
Worry:	Oh, He's here inside Joe, all right!
Fear:	So why isn't He at this meeting?
Worry:	He has no use for us!

Anger:	I know what He's doing. He's trying to snub us because we're the *established* Control Panel.
Worry:	Actually, to Him, we're just a bunch of control freaks!
Fear:	Okay. Then why do we have the controls right now? Huh?
Worry:	Apparently, Joe will soon learn what it is to not only receive the Holy Spirit, but how to be controlled by Him as well.
Flesh:	Then we're in big trouble. Joe's brought in the big guns. I've heard about the Holy Spirit! He's tough!
Fear:	Our battle is not with the Holy Spirit . . . it is with Joe. We need to always try to get to him before he hands the controls over to the Holy Spirit.
Anger:	And who says that Joe won't get tired of the guy after a while, anyway? I have a friend on Mr. Johnson's Control Panel, and he says that the Holy Spirit is there too, but Mr. Johnson rarely gives Him control.
Worry:	Let's just hope that Joe will fall into a spiritual rut or something.
SOUND	**MUSICAL TRANSITION OUT OF SKETCH**
Fear:	And until then . . . I say we let Joe have it!
Flesh:	Let's give him all we got!
Anger:	And all at once.
Worry:	'Cause you never know when life as we've known it with Joe will change.
Fear:	To your battle stations, men!
	(As music plays, the panel marches to the front of the table. ANGER takes the controls and hands them to the FLESH. The FLESH pushes the remote, smiles, and hands the remote off to FEAR. FEAR likewise pushes the remote, and then hands it to a nervous WORRY. All four then begin pushing buttons and laughing . . . enjoying what is happening to Joe)
LIGHTS:	**FADE TO BLACK**
	END

▸ *Caution:*
Seriously Not Funny

Be careful not to turn a serious sketch into a ridiculous comedy by overdeveloping the characterization of the roles. Real people can be characters (just go visit your local bus station), but if you go too far with accents or costumes, you will lose the message in the clutter of characterization.

OFF BROADWAY

TOPIC
Choosing between the "Broadway" and the "Narrow Way."

SCRIPTURE
Matthew 7:13-14

SYNOPSIS
An allegorical representation of man's decision to choose the Broadway which leads to destruction, or the narrow way which leads to life. A group of young actors are mesmerized by the lights of Broadway, where they hope to find fame, fortune, and happiness. When one of the actors chooses an off-Broadway run, the others try to pressure him into going with them to Broadway!

SETS/PROPS
No particular set is required. A street sign with arrows indicating "Broadway" and "Narrow Way" can be placed at the back of the stage. Each actor should wear the appropriate attire for a singing/dancing audition for a Broadway show. Gym bags, portfolios, etc., can be carried by the actors. VICTOR should have a portfolio of pictures or a resume.

CHARACTERS
Destiny – aspiring actress

Chance – aspiring actor

Hope – aspiring actress

Lucky – aspiring actor

Victor – actor

LIGHTS:	BLACKOUT *(Actors move into place)*
SOUND:	MUSICAL TRANSITION INTO SKETCH: BROADWAY FEEL
GRAPHIC:	TITLE SLIDE— *Off Broadway*
LIGHTS:	UP ON STAGE

(Lights come up on an empty stage. Then DESTINY, CHANCE, HOPE, LUCKY run onstage, looking out toward the audience with awe at seeing the lights of Broadway. VICTOR trails a little behind.)

Chance: We made it!

Destiny: Look at it! Isn't it beautiful?

Hope: Broadway!

Lucky: Wow! It's bigger than I had imagined!

Chance: Bigger! Brighter! And soon to be better, because we'll be stars on Broadway!

Destiny: *(Proudly)* We're ready for Broadway, but is Broadway ready for us?

Hope: Ready or not, here we come! Step aside, all you fledgling Broadway wannabes! The real performers have arrived!

Lucky: Just look at all that's going on! I want a piece of it all!

Destiny: Doesn't it look great, Victor?

Victor: Sure . . . I guess so.

Chance: Come on, Victor . . . this is what we've dreamed about! This is what we've always wanted. I'd think you'd be excited like the rest of us.

Victor: I'm sorry, Chance. Now that we're faced with life on Broadway, I guess I'm having second thoughts.

Lucky: Nothing to think twice about, buddy. Believe me, you want everything Broadway has to offer.

Hope: If you're going to really be somebody, it's got to happen here.

Destiny: *(To Victor)* C'mon, honey . . . I thought we talked this through. Everything's going to be fine.

(To the rest of the group) Hey, let's practice presenting ourselves to all those wonderful directors who could make us big stars!

Lucky: Yeah, when they find out who we are and what we've done, they'll grab us right up!

(The rest agree. One by one they present themselves . . .)

Chance: *(Steps forward, holds up a headshot and/or resume, and addresses an imaginary Broadway director)* Hello, I'm Chance. *(Refers to photos)* This is me . . . and this is me . . . me again . . . *(refers to resume)* . . . and this is all I've done. Impressive, huh? If you're looking for a leading man, no need to look any further. You see, I want the world to fall in love with me. I want to be a somebody! Help me be a somebody!

(Group applauds, ad-libs positive responses)

▶ *Drama Cue: Stark Realism*

An empty stage can be one of the most effective ways to transport your audience wherever you want them to go. A bare set will become a specific place as the dialogue unravels. The starkness can actually lend to the realism through imagination. Try performing this sketch without any set pieces.

Destiny: *(Stepping forward for her imaginary audition. Holds up resume)* I'm Destiny! What a wonderful name to see up in lights, don't you think?! Destiny! I'll do anything to be famous. I'll take any role. Play any part! With your direction and my talent, we'll be a hit!

(Again, group applauds and ad-libs positive response)

Lucky: I'm Lucky! I'm here to go for the lead in the new production called *Money*" I've been told that *Money* promises to be a hit, and I want to be a part of that cast! If *Money* can bring me the happiness and security I've always wanted, then I really will be "lucky" . . . get it? Hey . . . you can't go wrong with me . . . I feel lucky! You will, too. Pick me! What do you say?

(Group applauds)

Hope: I'm Hope! Hope you'll like me. Hope you'll choose me. Hope you'll make me a star! *(Holds up resume)* Hope you'll take the time to look over my resume. Hope you'll be impressed . . . most people are. Hope I'm doing the right thing. Hope all my dreams will come true! Hope Broadway's everything it's supposed to be. Hope I didn't say too much. Thank you!

(Group applauds)

Destiny: Okay, Victor, let's hear your audition.

Victor: I don't think I'm ready . . .

(Group ad-libs encouragement)

(Begins unenthusiastically) Hello, I'm Victor. And . . . and . . . forget it.

Chance: What's wrong?

Victor: Nothing.

Lucky: C'mon, Victor, what gives?

Victor: All right, I'll tell you. I don't want to be on Broadway!

Destiny: But it's always been our dream to play Broadway together!

Victor: I know that, Destiny, but I think I want to go off Broadway.

(Shocked, everyone reacts negatively)

Hope: Do you have any idea how difficult an off-Broadway run is?

Lucky: Nothing exciting happens there!

Chance: And you certainly won't draw the crowds or get the press like you will on Broadway!

Destiny: You have too much to offer than to waste it on an off-Broadway production!

Victor: Well, you see, I want to be in *Life*, and it's only running off-Broadway. Besides, I really believe in the Director and want to be a follower of His and to learn from Him.

▶ *Caution: Double Vision*

This script calls for the cast to look out over the audience at two specific areas. Designate two distinct spots in the back of the auditorium as focal points for Broadway and Off Broadway.

Lucky: Let me guess—another director who thinks he's God!

Victor: You guys want to see your name up in lights . . . I'd just like to see the Light. You want to be stars . . . I just want to be His understudy. You want the applause and cheers of men . . . I just want Him to congratulate me on a job well done.

Hope: But what if He doesn't want you?

Victor: What?

Hope: What if He rejects you?

Chance: Yeah, this Director might see you, look at what you've done, and then say, "Don't call us; we'll call you."

Lucky: Then you'll wish you chose Broadway!

(VICTOR sits in silence)

Destiny: Victor, you're making a big mistake.

Victor: Please come with me, Destiny. I know this way seems strange, but I know it's the right way.

Destiny: If you can be happy off-Broadway, that's fine . . . but I can't. Broadway is calling my name. *(DESTINY gives VICTOR a kiss on the cheek, then turns to the others)* C'mon, guys, let's go be stars!

SOUND: **MUSIC TRANSITION OUT OF SKETCH: QUIET/SENTIMENTAL**

(The group picks up their belongings and one by one leaves. After the last one leaves the stage, leaving VICTOR alone . . .)

LIGHTS: **FOLLOW SPOTS HIT VICTOR AS STAGE LIGHTS GO TO BLACK**

(VICTOR now stands in the spotlight. He looks up.)

Victor: Oh . . . it's You! Uh . . . I'm Victor. *(Pulls out portfolio)* This is me. And, uh . . . this is me.

(Looks up for any signs of approval) And this . . . and . . . *(Takes out resume)* These are all of the things I've done. I'm not proud of them, but nevertheless, I've done them. I thought you should know. I hope you'll take me. I know its off-Broadway. *(Brokenly)* I understand that the road is narrow and the run can be difficult. I don't care if I'm just an understudy, I just really want to . . .

(At first incredulous, and then with growing joy) What . . . I made it? You'll take me? I'm going to have a role in Life? I'm . . . in? I'm in!

FOLLOW SPOTS: **FADE TO BLACK**

END

United We Sit

TOPIC

Christian unity: There can be no unity where there is no humility.

STYLE

Comedy

SCRIPTURE

Ephesians 4

SYNOPSIS

Wally has just moved into town and found a new church. He has brought along quite a bit of baggage from his previous legalistic church, where members of the congregation were frequently subjected to judgment and humiliation. As Wally participates in his first committee meeting in his new church, he is defensive, touchy, and prepared to be mistreated. Imagine his surprise when he finds himself surrounded by open, caring, accepting Christians who act out of humility and love.

CAST

Wally – gun-shy; defensive; touchy; persecution complex; sensitive

Darla – church committee member

Alan – church committee member

Jean – church committee member

Opal – church committee member

Grant – church committee member

SETS/PROPS

The sketch takes place in a church meeting room with six chairs forming a semicircle. Props include meeting notes, pens, etc.

LIGHTS:	**BLACKOUT** *(Actors move into place)*
SOUND:	**MUSICAL TRANSITION INTO SKETCH**
GRAPHIC:	**TITLE SLIDE—** *United We Sit*
LIGHTS:	**UP ON STAGE**

(We see the cast sitting in a church meeting room with their chairs arranged in a semicircle. ALAN sits on one end and WALLY sits on the other with everyone else sitting between them. WALLY holds a stack of notes that he will pass out to the others.)

Alan: Thank you for coming out on a Tuesday night for this very special committee meeting. And, oh, Pastor Frank wanted me to extend his thanks to you as well.

(The group reacts with murmurs of humble grace and joy.)

Okay, now, the first thing I would like to do tonight is introduce our newest volunteer member of the Church Activities Committee, Wally Strangler.

(The committee claps.)

Wally: *(Very serious)* Thank you; I'm glad to be involved.

Darla: Wally just moved into town and comes highly recommended to us from another church.

Wally: *(Loudly and defensively)* Which is not exactly the same affiliation as this one, so if you have a beef with that, tell me right now! But I think there is room in heaven for all of us!

(The committee doesn't know what to think. They look at one another and then smile at Wally.)

Opal: *(Smiling)* No beef here. We're glad you're in our church.

Wally: Really? I mean, there's not going to be any discussion? Interrogation?

Jean: I think we're all fine.

Grant: Let's get down to business.

(WALLY is still a little wary.)

Alan: Well, as you are aware, we are here to talk about the all-church picnic. I hope you came with ideas on how we can make this picnic a great family event.

Wally: *(Energetically)* I came with some ideas. I made a copy for each of you. *(Begins to pass them down the row)* There are ideas for everything from food to games, music, and . . .

(Catches himself. Emotionally kicking himself . . .)

▸ *Drama Cue:*
Laughing at Ourselves

Church life can be humorous. When performing a drama that shows the sometimes wacky behavior of believers, keep the drama light and fun. You'll find your congregation will make the connection and laugh at themselves.

Oh, I am sorry! I'm the new guy here. I shouldn't have spoken first! You all are probably thinking, "Who does this guy think he is?" Sorry! Forgive me!

(WALLY begins to retrieve his handouts . . .)

Grant: Wally, it's okay. You can speak first.

Wally: But I'm the new guy.

Grant: So?

Wally: I'm at the bottom of the pecking order and I shouldn't have—

Darla: Wally, don't be silly! Let's see what you have.

(WALLY lets everyone read his notes. He sits at the edge of his chair, like he's waiting on a jury's decision in the courtroom.)

Opal: I see you have music written down here.

Wally: Okay, I knew it! Chew me up and spit me out just because I like a little toe-tapping Southern Gospel music!

Opal: No, I . . .

Wally: Look down your nose at me, but I think there's room in heaven for all of us, no matter what kind of music we like!

Opal: We love Southern Gospel music.

Wally: You do?

Opal: Yes.

Jean: *(Looking at handout)* and you have games listed here, like the three-legged race, egg toss, and volleyball.

Wally: Oh, I get what you're implying! You don't think I'm very spiritual because I like some good clean competition every once in a while.

Jean: Actually, I was . . .

Wally: Think me carnal, but I think there's room in heaven for all of us, even if some of us like sports!

Grant: Wally. Hey, we play games every year at the church picnic.

Jean: We've never played these games, though. They're great!

Wally: They are?

Alan: *(Looking at handout)* Puppet shows? Clowns? Balloon sculptures?

Wally: *(Once again defensive)* Yeah, what about them?

Alan: I was just . . .

Wally:	You were just calculating the depth of my spirituality because I suggested such frivolous, unspiritual activities for the kids!
Alan:	What I was going to say was . . .
Wally:	Think me spiritually shallow, but I think there's room in heaven for all of us, even if we like an occasional puppet show or silly balloon hat!
Alan:	Wally. Our kids will love this!
Darla:	You have some great ideas here.
Opal:	I'm impressed.
Jean:	Me, too.
Grant:	I move that we use all of Wally's suggestions for the church picnic!
Darla:	I second the motion.
Alan:	All in favor?
All:	*(Except Wally)* Aye!
Alan:	Opposed?
	(No one speaks.)
	So be it! Now, shall we talk about the food? Opal?
Opal:	The women of the church have filled the sign-up sheets for the potluck.
Wally:	Wait. Excuse me.
Alan:	Yes?
Wally:	What just happened here?
Darla:	What do you mean?
Wally:	No fighting? No name-calling? All in favor say "Aye" and you all said "Aye"?
Jean:	So?
Wally:	You're not going to judge me? No sermons to make me feel guilty about music, my hair, my clothes, or . . .
Darla:	Your shoes.
Wally:	What's wrong with my shoes?
Darla:	They're untied.
Wally:	Oh.
Alan:	Wally, I don't know what kind of church you came from, but at this church, we love and accept each other . . .

▸ *Caution: Church Separation*

Creating a scene from church life? Don't make the mistake of placing the sketch in your own church. Separate the plot, characters, and situation from anything going on in your own congregation. If the message of the drama hits too close to home, you don't want to be accused of taking jabs at people. Keep your pastor and parishioners out of the storyline.

Jean:	*. . . and* our silly little differences.
Grant:	Unity is huge to us, and we do whatever we can to keep it that way.
Opal:	We love you, Wally, and we are glad you're here. Your unique individuality brings a whole new dimension to our congregation.
Darla:	And we love your ideas for the picnic.
SOUND:	**MUSICAL TRANSITION OUT OF SKETCH**
	(WALLY is stunned.)
Alan:	Meeting adjourned.
	(Everyone except WALLY stands, collects their things, and begins to head out of the meeting room. Before they leave the room they realize WALLY is still sitting.)
Darla:	Wally? The meeting is over.
Wally:	Back at my old church, I was always the last one to leave the room. That way I would know . . .
Opal:	That no one was talking about you after you left the room?
Wally:	Uh-huh.
Alan:	Wally, united we sit and united we stand! C'mon, let's grab a pizza!
Wally:	*(Standing, adds a warning)* Okay, but I don't eat meat!
All:	*(Smiling, but firm)* C'mon!
	MUSIC SWELLS
	(A happy WALLY joins the group as they exit together.)
LIGHTS:	**FADE TO BLACK**
	END

WHAT'S UP WITH JACK?

TOPIC
Evidence of conversion

SYNOPSIS
Jack's friends and family have hired a detective to find Jack!
His sudden departure has them worried. In fact, for the past six weeks
Jack's been different. His mother, girlfriend, buddy, and boss all attest to
Jack's "new behavior," and are worried something is wrong. When the
detective puts all the evidence together, they realize that Jack's become
a Christian . . . and is off to Mexico on a mission trip.

SETS/PROPS
Characters can sit or stand. A box is needed.
Inside the box, place these things:
- CD
- A Bible with a colored flyer inside
- A devotional book

CHARACTERS

Detective – serious, analytical

Mrs. Baker – Jack's concerned mother

Dawn – Jack's girlfriend

Sammy – Jack's buddy

Mr. Wells – Jack's supervisor

LIGHTS:	**BLACKOUT** *(Actors move into place)*
MUSIC:	**TRANSITION MUSIC INTO SKETCH**
GRAPHIC:	**TITLE SLIDE—** *What's Up with Jack?*
LIGHTS:	**UP ON STAGE**

(We see DAWN, SAMMY, and MR. WELLS all gathered around MOM in a frenzied discussion. DETECTIVE saunters in ... Gives them a once over then crosses to them.)

▸ *Drama Cue: Ensemble Casts*

Ensemble sketches are a perfect way to demonstrate a variety of approaches to one idea or topic. You'll find that your audience relates well to ensembles because everyone can find a character who treats the subject as they would.

Detective:	Mrs. Baker?
Mrs. Baker:	*(Turning)* Yes? Oh! You must be the detective I sent for. Am I glad to see you! Well, I just didn't know what to do . . . you know he's gone, and we . . .

(The others join in trying to give the DETECTIVE the story)

Detective:	Hold it! Hold on, here! One at a time. Let's start from the beginning. What's the problem here?
Mrs. Baker:	Jack . . . he's gone.
Detective:	Who's Jack?
Mrs. Baker:	My son!
Dawn:	My ex-boyfriend!
Sammy:	My friend!
Mr. Wells:	My employee!
Detective:	And he's gone?
Mrs. Baker:	That's right . . . and we're very concerned about him!
Detective:	Do you know where he went?
Dawn:	Yes . . .
All:	Mexico!
Detective:	*(Wondering)* So if you all know he's in Mexico, why are you so worried about him being gone?
Mrs. Baker:	When I found out he was in Mexico, that's when I began to worry!
Detective:	What do you mean?
Dawn:	The reason Jack's mom is so worried is because Jack has a history of drug use!
Detective:	Oh, I see.
Buddy:	Jack's had a lot of problems where that is concerned . . . until recently.

Detective:	What do you mean, until recently?
Buddy:	Jack used to be the coolest guy. We'd hang out, you know, paint the town red . . . sometimes do a little drugs . . . but he suddenly quit hanging out with me and the rest of the guys about six weeks ago.
Dawn:	And that was about the time he came to me and told me that our relationship had to change. Out of the clear blue he announces that we weren't going to be intimate anymore, and that we needed to plan on getting married.
Detective:	So what did you do?
Dawn:	I broke up with him! I'm not ready for marriage!
Detective:	So he did change his mind?
Dawn:	No. I spent a couple weeks trying to wear him down, but he was adamant about his decision.
Mr. Wells:	I noticed a change in Jack's behavior about the same time, too. He started showing up to work on time, did his job and walked around with a smile on his face. I just thought he was perpetually high or something.
Mrs. Baker:	Jack and I used to argue a lot. We'd scream at each other, call one another names! Boy, did that boy have a mouth on him!
Detective:	*Did* have a mouth?
Mrs. Baker:	That's right. He's been so respectful to me of late that I think he might be sick or something!
Detective:	Anything else in his behavior that's been different?
Dawn:	Well, like his mom said, he's cleaned up his language!
Sammy:	And his house!
Mr. Wells:	And his jokes!
Mrs. Baker:	Detective, my son has slowly declined during the past six weeks! I know something's wrong. I used to call him every Sunday morning and check on him, you know, make sure he made it home from the night before . . . but for the last few weeks, he doesn't answer . . . he's not at home!
Detective:	I understand what you are saying, but it sounds to me like all the changes in Jack's life have been positive changes.
Dawn:	Thanks a lot.
Detective:	With all due respect, Jack wanted a change.
Sammy:	You're telling me . . . I don't even know the guy anymore.
Mr. Wells:	Yeah, really! He must have been on something the day he asked me to go to church with him!

▸ *Caution: Hot Dogging*

Some actors have a tough time being a part of an ensemble cast. There is a tendency for actors to want to give more than what the script calls for, "hot dogging" for attention through over-the-top characterization. Actors need to be taught that blending in with the crowd is sometimes the most effective way to get the message across to the audience.

Dawn:	Me, too! That was part of the new deal!
Sammy:	He wanted me to go, too!
Mrs. Baker:	See, my son's probably in Mexico in some sort of cult or something . . .
Detective:	When I talked to you on the phone, I asked if you would check his apartment and bring me any items that might gives us clues to what he's doing.
Mrs. Baker:	We did that. *(Opens the box)* We found some really weird stuff. First of all, *(pulls out a CD)* a CD . . . from some band called Promise Keepers!
Sammy:	I think they're a heavy metal group!
Detective:	Promise Keepers, huh?
Mrs. Baker:	Then we found this on his bed. *(Hands the DETECTIVE the devotional)*
Detective:	*(Scrutinizes the cover, then reads the title)* A *Man of Conviction* daily devotional.
Dawn:	That book ruined our relationship!
Mrs. Baker:	And then this . . . *(pulls out a Bible)* A . . . Bible!
	(Everyone is puzzled)
Detective:	Let me see it.
	(The DETECTIVE thinks hard . . . then begins flipping through the Bible and finds the flyer about Mexico. Reads the flyer without showing the others, who are in deep consternation)
	I know what's up with Jack!
Mrs. Baker:	*(Surprised)* You do?
Dawn:	Already?
Mr. Wells:	Man, you're good.
Sammy:	So what do you think?
Detective:	Well, from all the testimony and evidence you gave me, it's clear that about six weeks ago Jack became a Christian.
All:	A Christian?!
Detective:	Of course. Look at the great changes that took place in his life. He was in God's house on Sunday morning and he quit the drinking and the drugs! His language, his morals, and his work ethic are all different now. He's reading the Bible and spending time in God's Word. He's not high on drugs; he's high on his new life in Christ!
Mrs. Baker:	But that doesn't explain why he's off to Mexico!

Detective:	No, but this does. *(He holds up the colored flyer)* A mission trip to Mexico!
Dawn:	What?
Mrs. Baker:	With the church?
Sammy:	Are you sure?
Detective:	It says right here . . . they left yesterday and will be back . . .
Mrs. Baker:	On Saturday . . . he said that on my machine. And here I thought he was up to no good . . .
Detective:	Let me tell you something, the Jack you knew is no longer. But the new Jack, the Jack that is at peace with himself, is down in Mexico spreading the joy of the Lord.
	(Everyone stops for a second)
Mrs. Baker:	Wow, do I ever feel silly!
Sammy:	I shouldn't have doubted him.
Mr. Wells:	I like the new Jack!
	(Everyone looks at DAWN)
Dawn:	I'm just trying to get used to the marriage or nothing part . . .
	(MOM, DAWN, SAMMY, and MR. WELLS return to the huddle and talk. The DETECTIVE walks out to address the audience)
MUSIC:	**MUSIC TRANSITION OUT OF THE SKETCH**
	Another missing persons case solved. Jack sounds like a good guy, and I really believe his conversion was sincere. How do I know that? *(Points to the others)* They're the proof . . . they don't know Jack anymore. Case closed. I love it when they end this way!
LIGHTS:	**FADE TO BLACK**
	END

© 2006 Paul Joiner - Please see page iv for more information.

You Need an Upgrade!

(Reader's Theater)

TOPIC

Law versus grace

SCRIPTURE

Galatians 3:1-5

SYNOPSIS

A woman's friends accuse her of being out-of-date. They criticize her house, her car, and her image. She willingly makes the changes they advocate, but she puts her foot down when they tell her she needs to upgrade her standing with God by works.

SET/PROPS

Stools for characters

CHARACTERS

Sylvia

Person 1

Person 2

Person 3

Person 4

LIGHTS:	**BLACKOUT** *(Actors move into place)*
MUSIC:	**TRANSITION INTO SKETCH**
GRAPHIC:	**TITLE SLIDE—** *You Need an Upgrade!*
LIGHTS:	**UP ON SET**
Sylvia:	*(Lifts her head and begins talking directly to the audience)* I have always made an effort to keep up with the times. I'm well read and up-to-date on current events. In general, I thought I had a decent grasp on what life was all about. But you know how it goes . . . as soon as you learn to play the game, the rules change. And it seems that as soon as you get your act together, the show closes.

Anyway, I was very happy with my life until recently. That's when my bubble burst . . .

(PERSONS 1 through 4 lift their heads . . .) |
Persons 1 to 4:	Sylvia, you need an upgrade!
Sylvia:	An upgrade?
Person 1:	Yes, an upgrade. Just look at this place.
Sylvia:	You don't like my house?
Person 1:	It's a little out-of-date.
Sylvia:	What is it, the avocado-green shag carpet?
Person 1:	Exactly . . . besides clashing with the bright orange macramé pots, it fights with the Bible-character-painted-on-velvet series you have hanging in your den.
Sylvia:	Oh . . .
Person 1:	It's like you're stuck in a bad episode of *The Brady Bunch*. You need to recarpet the floors . . .
Person 2:	Put in a skylight or two . . .
Person 3:	Put chrome appliances in the kitchen . . .
Person 4:	Get rid of the doughboy and put in a Jacuzzi!
Sylvia:	Well, the house could use some remodeling. Maybe you're right.
Person 1:	Believe me, Sylvia . . . we're right!

(PERSONS 1 to 4 drop their heads . . .) |
| **Sylvia:** | And so I remodeled! The house looked terrific, and I felt a great sense of accomplishment. That was, until . . .

(PERSONS 1 to 4 lift their heads again . . .) |
| **Persons 1 to 4:** | Sylvia, you need an upgrade! |

▶ *Drama Cue: Reader's Theater*

When performing a Reader's Theater piece, have your actors stand or sit on stools. They should hold their script in one hand and use the other to gesture and turn pages. Actors should direct their dialogue toward the audience even though they are speaking to one another. Find placement for each actor across the auditorium when talking to a specific character.

Sylvia:	I thought I just had one!
Person 2:	Now that your house looks acceptable, it's time to trade in that old station wagon for a minivan!
Sylvia:	But my station wagon does the job just fine!
Person 2:	Sylvia, no one drives a station wagon anymore. Minivans can accommodate the whole family . . . they have plenty of room . . . and they're great for shopping.
Sylvia:	My station wagon does all that!
Person 2:	But does it have individual Nintendo stations built into every seat?
Person 3:	Does it have a mini washer and dryer in the back to wash little uniforms as you go to and from the kids' games?
Person 4:	Or an espresso machine in the center console and a yogurt maker in the glove box?
Person 1:	I bet your station wagon isn't cable ready!
Sylvia:	No, it's not . . . but it does have that nice wood-grain contact paper running along the sides.
	(PERSONS 1 to 4 look at SYLVIA . . . look back at the audience . . . and drop their heads.)
	So I got a mini-van, complete with Dolby surround sound in back for the kids. The very next week I was attending a Parents with Minivans support group, feeling pretty good about myself, when I heard it again . . .
Persons 1 to 4:	Sylvia, you need an upgrade!
Sylvia:	I'm not hauling the kids around in an SUV!
Person 3:	It's not that.
Sylvia:	What is it then? My yard? My cooking? My dental work?
Person 3:	Your image.
Sylvia:	My what?
Person 3:	You need to upgrade your wardrobe. You look like you're . . .
Sylvia:	I know . . . I look like I'm stuck in a bad episode of *The Brady Bunch* . . .
Person 3:	I was thinking more of *The Addams Family* . . .
Sylvia:	You were?
Person 3:	You need to have your colors done!
Sylvia:	Ooh, that sounds painful! Does it hurt?

Person 3:	No, silly . . . it will tell you how to coordinate your wardrobe to emphasize your best features. For instance, I'm a winter . . .
Person 4:	I'm a spring . . .
Person 2:	I'm a summer . . .
Person 1:	And I'm an autumn . . .
Sylvia:	And here I thought the rule was that if it didn't rip when you sat down, it was okay to wear it.
Person 3:	Sylvia, after we upgrade your wardrobe, we'll work on your hair and makeup.
Sylvia:	*(Sarcastically)* I can't wait.
	(PERSONS 1 to 4 drop their heads . . .)
	After that little incident, I thought I was ready for them. I made a list of everything everybody was doing nowadays and set out to become a twenty-first century woman. I bungee jumped off a neighbor's ham-radio antenna. I started drinking fancy coffees with names I couldn't pronounce. I became politically active and even joined a nationwide women's movement— scrapbooking! How more well-rounded, progressive, and up-to-date can you get?
	(PERSONS 1 to 4 lift their heads . . .)
Persons 1 to 4:	Sylvia, you need an upgrade!
Sylvia:	I give up!
Person 4:	We're a little concerned for you.
Sylvia:	Not the right shade of lipstick, huh?
Person 4:	This is much more important than lipstick.
Sylvia:	Sounds serious.
Person 4:	It's your spiritual condition.
Sylvia:	What about my spiritual condition?
Persons 1 to 4:	It's time for an upgrade.
Sylvia:	I'm not following you.
Person 4:	What are you doing to upgrade your standing with God?
Sylvia:	I was saved by grace . . .
Person 4:	But what's keeping you in His favor?
Sylvia:	Huh?
Person 4:	What are you doing to keep acceptable in the sight of God . . . you know, to be found worthy of your salvation?

▸ *Caution: Burled in Your Script*

Though a script *is* used in a Reader's Theater presentation, actors should only refer to it from time to time . . . usually during another actor's lines. Having your face buried in your script defeats the purpose of Reader's Theater.

Person 1:   To secure your home in heaven!

Person 2:   To be transported to glory!

Person 3:   To be adorned with a crown of life!

Person 4:   To know that, by your deeds, God is pleased with you and your place with Him is secure.

Sylvia: *(To audience)* I couldn't believe what I was hearing. Upgrade my standing with God? Enough was enough!

(Preaching to PERSONS 1 to 4) Listen here, I have remodeled the house and traded in the station wagon . . . I even had my upper lip waxed! All to become a better, more "upstanding" person.

But there is nothing that I can do, save for what Jesus Christ did on the cross for me, that will ever make me more acceptable to God than I already am! Rules, regulations, and other Christians' personal opinions won't change that. When I choose to do something that is pleasing to God, it is because I love Him and want to serve Him . . . It is not to secure my relationship with Him . . . because you see, without the blood of Jesus, all my righteousness is as "filthy rags"!

(Pause . . .)

Person 1:   If that's the way you feel. *(Drops head)*

Person 2:   Excuses, Sylvia, excuses. *(Drops head)*

Person 3:   Gotta go! *(Drops head)*

Person 4:   Good luck! *(Drop head)*

MUSIC: **SOFT BACKGROUND MUSIC TO PLAY TO END AND TRANSITION OUT**

Sylvia: "Good luck"! It's like they're stuck in a bad episode of Bewitched.

(Looks up to heaven) God, thank You for sending Your Son, Jesus Christ, to accomplish something I could never do . . . be holy in Your sight. You accept me because of Him. There's no way I could upgrade that! Some things better left alone. Thank You!

(Drops head.)

LIGHTS: **FADE TO BLACK**

END

You've Got the Whole World in Your Hands

TOPIC
Loving the things of the world

SCRIPTURE
1 John 2:15-17

SYNOPSIS
A woman struggles with desiring things of the world. In this scenario, the woman agonizes over whether she wants to buy "the world," which is on display in a fine department store. (NOTE: Any of these characters can be played by male or female; names just need to be changed.)

SETS/PROPS
A column or pedestal with a globe sitting on it, covered with a scarf or large napkin (prior to the performance, the globe will need to be cut in half along the equator); a hand-held mirror; two bags, one gold and one silver; a few artificial potted plants (optional); and a second globe.

CHARACTERS
Jan – customer

Salesman

Gloria – Jan's friend

LIGHTS:	BLACKOUT *(Actors move into place)*
MUSIC:	MUSIC TRANSITION INTO SKETCH
GRAPHIC:	TITLE SLIDE— *You've Got the Whole World In Your Hands*
LIGHTS:	UP ON STAGE

(A short column or pedestal is set CS; a globe is sitting on the column covered by a cloth. There is not much else around . . . maybe a few plants to give the scene a department store feel.)

(JAN enters. She is wearing sunglasses and a scarf tied around her head; she is trying to be inconspicuous. She casually looks around the store for a bit. Finally the SALESMAN enters. He notices JAN looking around. He smiles, knowing exactly why she is there. He crosses to her . . .)

Salesman: Hello there. May I help you with something?

Jan: *(Nervously)* Oh, no . . . no . . . just looking!

Salesman: Oh, really? I bet I know what you're looking for.

(The SALESMAN walks over to the pedestal and carefully removes the drape, revealing a beautiful globe sitting on the stand.)

Jan: *(Gasps with delight)* The world! It's beautiful! How did you know what I was looking for?

Salesman: *(Sarcastically)* With that disguise? I had you pegged the minute you walked in the door.

Jan: Well, you're right. I was looking for the world, but I didn't want anyone to see me.

Salesman: Understandable. Buying into the world should be a personal decision, don't you think?

Jan: Uh . . . yes, I think it should be.

Salesman: *(Folding the drape, referring to the world)* So you love it, or what?

Jan: I'm not sure I love it . . . maybe a little intrigued by it, though. It just seems so appealing.

Salesman: Nah . . . you love it. I can see it in your eyes. You want to take it home with you?

Jan: No . . . I just need a few minutes to think about it. Alone!

Salesman: Okay, just give me a holler when you need me.

(SALESMAN busies himself . . . maybe even exits the stage. JAN walks from side to side, keeping her distance from the globe but carefully examining it all the while.)

▸ *Drama Cue:*
Object Lesson

A drama performed around specific props is an object lesson. Each prop featured in a script represents something specific. Actors should understand that the props are every bit as meaningful as their dialogue.

(GLORIA enters. She has been shopping and quickly walks across the stage . . . she passes JAN and almost exits the other side of the stage when she stops dead in her tracks and turns to JAN.)

Gloria: Jan?

(JAN sees GLORIA and fumbles with her sunglasses to get them back on . . .)

Jan, is that you?

Jan: *(Feigning surprise)* Oh . . . Gloria? I didn't see you.

Gloria: Good to see you! How've you been?

Jan: *(Nervously)* I'm . . . fine . . . just fine. Well, good talking to you. Good-bye. *(Begins to leave)*

Gloria: Doing a little shopping, are you?

Jan: A little.

Gloria: *(Noticing the world)* You weren't looking at that, were you?

Jan: Looking at what?

Gloria: *(Pointing)* That . . . the world!

Jan: World . . . what world?

Gloria: The one right in front of your face.

Jan: Oh, **that** world! Looking at it? Me? Interested in the world? C'mon, Gloria you know me better than that!

Gloria: Well, I was a little worried there for a second. I had a friend who bought into the world, and boy, did he ever get messed up!

Jan: *(First signs of sincerity with Gloria)* He did?

Gloria: Yes. It's a tragic story. You know, it's hard not be tempted by the world. Everywhere you go the world is on display. I tell you, it takes a determined Christian not to give in.

Jan: I know what you mean.

Gloria: Hey, I've got to run. Good to see you, Jan. Listen . . . I wouldn't hang around the world too much longer *(pointing)* . . . Before you know it, you'll be embracing it.

See you.

(GLORIA exits)

Jan: *(Staring at world)* See you, Gloria.

(SALESMAN enters and crosses to JAN)

Salesman: *(Prodding her)* You want it. I can see it in your eyes!

Jan:	It *is* beautiful to look at.
Salesman:	Look at, nothing! There's more to the world than meets the eye. Let me show you what's in the world . . . *(SALESMAN walks over to the world and removes the top)* The world is more than what you see . . . it's what you get.
Jan:	What's in there?
Salesman:	Let's start with these two . . . *(He picks up the gold and silver bags)*
Jan:	*(Expressing her approval)* Oooh!
Salesman:	I knew you'd like them; most people do. These are the lust of the flesh and the lust of the eyes.
Jan:	*(Impressed, still intimidated)* Wow.
Salesman:	There's more in the world. Take a look at this . . . *(SALESMAN hands JAN an ornate hand-held mirror. JAN looks at herself in the mirror . . . a gentle smile crosses her face, as if she likes what she sees.)* That's the pride of life. *(JAN realizes what the mirror implies and moves it away.)*
Jan:	*(Placing the mirror back in the world)* All that is in there, huh?
Salesman:	That's right. *(Places the bags back in the half globe . . . then, as he speaks, replaces the top and puts the entire globe in JAN's hands)* It's one big package. Now, do you want to take the world home with you today?
Jan:	*(JAN stares at the globe she is holding)* I don't see a price tag . . . is it free?
Salesman:	*(Snaps at JAN)* No, don't be ridiculous! The world's going to cost you.
Jan:	Can I bring it back if I'm not happy?
Salesman:	Sorry, what's done is done. *(Scratching his head)* Though I have heard of someone who can help you get rid of the world, but you're on your own as far as I am concerned.
Jan:	I see.
Salesman:	So what will it be, ma'am? The world is in your hands.
SOUND:	**MUSICAL TRANSITION OUT OF SKETCH**
Jan:	*(Quietly struggles to decide, then recklessly makes her decision)* Okay, all right, I'll take it!
Salesman:	You want to take it as is?

▸ *Caution: Prop Shop*

When the foundation of a sketch is its props, do everything in your power to find the right ones. Last-minute searches usually turn up items that are not functional, believable, or professional; this will kill a prop-specific drama. Take the time to prop shop!

Jan: No! I want you to put it in a bag . . . a big bag . . . cover it with tissue paper . . . cover it up . . .

Salesman: *(Begins packing up the world)* I understand.

Jan: *(Fumbling in her purse)* How much do I owe you for it?

Salesman: *(Handing her the bag)* Take it now . . . you'll pay later. Enjoy the world.

Jan: *(Putting her sunglasses back on)* Thank you . . . I think . . .

(JAN exits. SALESMAN smiles. He then goes to the side and picks up another globe. Dusts it off a bit. Then carefully, like it is a museum piece, places it on the pedestal where the first globe sat. He then takes the drape . . . and spreads it gently over the globe.)

(Smiling) It looks like it's going to be a good day after all.

LIGHTS: FADE TO BLACK

END

Sally's Card Table

TOPIC
Marriage: Forgiveness

SYNOPSIS
A young married couple is embroiled in a stand-off over differences in their relationship. A family member steps in and takes the young couple on a field trip to Sally's house. Sally sits at her card table putting together a puzzle and is surrounded by wonderful greeting cards given to her by her husband. The young couple imagines that Sally has a wonderful relationship with her husband, but are surprised when they realize that Sally is alone. There was one card Sally kept while she was married, a scorecard, and it was ultimately her practice of keeping score that drove her husband away. If Sally had to do it all over again, she would not keep track of marital rights and wrongs, but live with a forgiving spirit.

CAST

Sally – 50s to 60s; kind; loving; broken; lonely

Judy – 50s to 60s; Shannon's aunt; spiritual; loving

Shannon – 20s; idealistic; stubborn; Eddie's wife

Eddie – 20s; idealistic; stubborn; Shannon's husband

SETS/PROPS
Sketch takes place in Sally's low-income home. Props needed are a card table, two chairs, a puzzle, and a dozen greeting cards.

LIGHTS:	**BLACKOUT** *(Actors move into place)*
SOUND:	**MUSICAL TRANSITION INTO SKETCH**
GRAPHIC:	**TITLE SLIDE—** *Sally's Card Table*
LIGHTS:	**UP ON STAGE**

(We see SALLY at a card table in her low-income home. She is dressed very plainly and is under-made-up. She sits down at a card table that has a dozen worn greeting cards and a puzzle on it. After a few moments JUDY, SHANNON, and EDDIE enter the door.)

Judy: Hello? Anyone home?

Sally: Oh yes! You know where to find me.

(JUDY, SHANNON, and EDDIE enter. SHANNON and EDDIE, a young couple, don't look very excited to be there and are not very pleasant to each other.)

Judy: Sally, thank you for letting us stop by on such short notice.

Sally: I sit here all day by myself. I was happy to hear you wanted to come by.

Judy: Well, let me introduce you to my niece, Shannon, and her husband, Eddie.

(SHANNON and EDDIE both say "hello" somewhat sullenly)

They've been married about three years now.

Sally: Your aunt has told me so much about you. I feel like I almost know you. May I offer you some tea?

Eddie: *(Uninterested)* No, thank you! We can't stay very long.

Shannon: Don't be rude, Eddie.

Eddie: *(Defensive)* I'm not!

Judy: *(Jumping in)* Uh, kids, Sally is the one who just gave me that framed puzzle.

Sally: Do you like it?

Judy: I hung it in my den.

Sally: I was just getting ready to start a new puzzle. I can do one a week now.

Judy: Sally, as I told you on the phone, Shannon and Eddie are having some serious marriage problems. They came to me for a little help, and I thought in light of what they were going through, it would be good for them to meet you.

Sally: So what seems to be the problem?

▸ *Drama Cue: Focal Point*

If a sketch has a specific focal point, such as a piece of furniture, a door, or a window, try making that the only set piece onstage. For example, if the family dinner table represents the lack of family time spent together, then don't clutter the stage with other pieces of furniture. Allow the audience to see the table for what it represents in the greater context of the drama.

Eddie:	It's Shannon . . . she can't let things go. She's constantly reminding me of mistakes I've made, even when I say I'm sorry.
Shannon:	Maybe so, but Eddie is stubborn and stuck in his ways. It's his way, or no way!
Sally:	I see.
Judy:	Sally, who do they remind you of?
Sally:	My husband and me.
Shannon:	Oh, so you understand what I'm going through!
Sally:	Yes. And what Eddie's going through, too.
Shannon:	That surprises me.
Sally:	Why?
Shannon:	All the cards on your table. They're beautiful! Are they from your husband?
Sally:	Yes. All given to me through the years.
Eddie:	Wow, what a romantic. *(Looking at the cards)* Valentine's Day cards! Anniversary cards! "Just Because I love you" cards.
Shannon:	Look at this one, an "I'm sorry" card. Wow, what a guy.
Sally:	Yeah, he was quite a guy. I really miss him.
Shannon:	Miss him?
	(SALLY nods.)
Eddie:	I'm sorry you're alone.
Sally:	Me too. We used to sit here at this card table and do these puzzles together. We'd laugh and talk all night. We had a terrific marriage. That is, until . . .
Shannon:	. . . he passed away. So that's why you're all alone.
Eddie:	How long ago did your husband pass away?
Sally:	My husband didn't pass away. I drove him away.
Shannon:	What?
SOUND:	**BACKGROUND MUSICAL BED**
Sally:	*(Referring to the cards on the table)* You noticed all these beautiful cards on my table. Well, there is another card I used to keep out here in the open when I was married to Jack.
Shannon:	What kind of card was that?
Sally:	A score card.
Eddie:	A score card?

51

Sally:	Yes. I may have loved Jack, but I couldn't forgive him. And even when I said I forgave him, I don't think I really meant it. I kept a running tally of all the things he did wrong. I kept a record of all the things I didn't get from him.
Shannon:	But your husband must have made some pretty big mistakes.
Sally:	You'd think so, wouldn't you? *(Thinking and getting emotional)* Actually, it was me. I graded him too harshly. I was too stubborn to forgive. Too bullheaded to let go. Too critical drawing comparisons between him and other husbands. It ultimately drove him away.
	(SHANNON and EDDIE don't know what to say.)
Judy:	Kids, Sally said she would tell you her story in hopes that it might help you two see what could happen if you continue down the road you're on.
Sally:	You see, I used to have the man who wrote these cards sitting here at my table with me. Now I have only his cards, but not him.
Eddie:	*(After a moment)* And the score card? Where is it?
Sally:	I finally let go of it a few years ago. If **only** I would have let go of it before my husband let go of me.
	MUSIC FADES
	(Silence for a moment . . .)
Judy:	Sally, thank you. We'll go now.
Sally:	*(Still staring at her cards)* Oh, come back any time.
Shannon:	*(Walks over and puts her hand on SALLY's shoulder)* Thank you so much for sharing your story.
Sally:	Throw that scorecard away. *(SHANNON nods)* And you throw yours away too. *(EDDIE nods)*
Eddie:	Maybe we'll come back one day and help you with your puzzle.
Sally:	There's always plenty of room at my card table.
SOUND:	**MUSICAL TRANSITION OUT OF SKETCH**
	(JUDY motions for the kids to leave. The kids begin to exit, and then embrace. They then wave good-bye to SALLY and exit arm in arm. JUDY follows the kids out. SALLY thoughtfully rearranges and straightens out her cards, then opens the puzzle and begins to work it . . .)
LIGHTS:	**FADE TO BLACK**
	END

▸ *Caution: Normalcy*

When a comedy takes a serious turn, be sure your actors practice transitioning smoothly. You already know how the sketch starts and how it will end; work at making the journey believable so that the audience can experience the story along with the characters.

THE PRAYER PANIC ATTACK

TOPIC
Prayer/praising God for His greatness enables us to see Him as a
God who can handle the problems of our lives.

SYNOPSIS
A group of individuals have been discussing their problems and feel that the
best thing they can do is to go before the Lord in prayer. One by one they
begin praying worrisome prayers, until panic begins to spread throughout
the circle. Finally the prayer meeting comes to a halt because they've
convinced themselves that God is unable to care for all their needs. Perhaps
if they had started by praising and acknowledging God as omnipotent and
omnipresent before they began petitioning Him, they would have seen that
they have a mighty God who can handle each of their problems.

SET/PROPS
Sketch can take place either in someone's home, or in a meeting/Sunday
school room. Characters should carry Bibles, notebooks, prayer lists, etc.

CHARACTERS
David

Casey

Karen

Jerry

Lynn

LIGHTS:	BLACKOUT *(Actors move into place)*
SOUND:	MUSIC TRANSITION INTO SKETCH
GRAPHIC:	SLIDE 1— *Have you ever been on your knees praying . . . when you've experienced a PPA?*
	SLIDE 2— *A Prayer Panic Attack!*
LIGHTS:	UP ON STAGE

(A prayer and Bible study group is in the midst of taking prayer requests. David somewhat facilitates the meeting and Casey is writing down the prayer requests.)

David: All right, Jerry, we are going to pray that your business picks up.

Jerry: Yeah, or I'll have to file bankruptcy.

David: Anyone else? No? Okay, Casey, could you review the prayer requests that have been mentioned so far?

Casey: *(Reading off list)* David, you asked for prayer concerning your medical tests, which you will receive results for on Wednesday. And you're having some struggles dealing with your business partner. Karen, you're concerned about how to juggle work, home, and school.

Karen: Yes, and don't forget I need a new place to live by the thirtieth! Which is Wednesday!

Casey: That's right. Okay, Lynn. We're praying for her sinuses, her conflict with her mother, aunt, and sister . . . and she asked us to remember world peace.

Lynn: Thank you.

Casey: Jerry, you need your business to start doing better . . .

Jerry: Yeah . . . or I'm ruined. I'm having a little stomach trouble as well. Going to the doctor this week about that . . . while I've still got insurance.

Casey: Okay. And I requested prayer because I'm having car problems and have no money for repairs.

David: A long list today. Well, let's go to the Lord with our petitions.

(Everyone bows their head to pray. It is silent for a second.)

Lynn: Oh Father, the world is in such terrible shape. With war and fighting in the Middle East and Europe, and the unrest on our own borders! What will become of this world?

David: And even at home we pray for those who are being afflicted by forest fires raging out of control. And for those who are being besieged by the devastating hurricanes on our coasts!

▸ *Drama Cue:*
Spice of Life

Ensemble casts often contain a variety of different but interesting characters. When there is no one lead in the sketch, adding creative touches to each cast member's role will make the drama much more memorable.

Casey:	And what about all these unknown viruses that are cropping up all over the place? Keep us safe from these, Lord.
Jerry:	Keep us safe on our city streets, too, where violence and crime run rampant.
	(Whining/worrisome prayer begins)
Karen:	But Father, with all You have to do in the world, please don't forget that you've got to help me know how to juggle my time between school and work . . . and I need someplace to live . . . by the thirtieth, you know . . . which is Wednesday.
David:	Speaking of Wednesday, don't forget that I need You there with me when I go to the doctor's for my medical workup . . . Wednesday.
Jerry:	And my stomach appointment is Wednesday, too, Father.
	(JERRY, DAVID, and KAREN all look up during prayer and at one another)
Lynn:	My sinuses, Lord. My sinuses!
Casey:	A car, Father! Where is it going to come from?
David:	Convict my business partner!
	(The group is beginning their "panic attack.")
Lynn:	Convict my mother, aunt, and sister! Convict them all!
Jerry:	Lord, you've got to send someone in to help save my business!
Casey:	Money. Where's it going to come from?
Lynn:	Let there be peace on earth!
Casey:	*(Halting the prayer)* Wait! Wait!
	(Everyone looks up from having worked themselves into a panic.)
David:	What's wrong?
Casey:	I'm having one of those prayer panic attacks again!
Jerry:	Yeah, me too!
Karen:	I'm freaking out!
Casey:	How can He do it, huh? I mean, look at all God has to be on top of! My problems, your problems, the world's problems!
Karen:	That's right! God has to find me an apartment, go with you to the doctor, and go with you to the doctor—all on Wednesday. How's He going to pull that off?
Lynn:	And I just remembered I'm having lunch with my mother on Wednesday!

> *Caution:*
> *Stay on Message*

Have fun creating characters in this sketch, but don't let the characterizations overshadow the message of the piece. You want the audience to laugh at the situation being presented, not at an outlandish cast that upstages the message. This is particularly important when the sketch ends on a serious tone.

Jerry:	Look how big our problems are! And we're just five people! God's got the whole world to keep track of! Someone or something's going to slip through the cracks!
David:	But God can handle all of this! He hears each of our prayers!
Casey:	But what chance do I have? What is more important, forest fires or a new radiator?
Lynn:	Sinuses or world peace? Sinuses? World peace? I know where I stand!
David:	All right, everyone, calm down. No need to panic. We serve a very big God! We've got ourselves all worked up about our problems, and we're praying like we don't believe God can handle it. Now, everyone take a deep breath.
	(Breath)
Casey:	Why do I get these panic attacks?
Karen:	I always end up freaking out when I place my petitions before the Lord!
David:	I think I know why. We forgot the praise.
Jerry:	Praise?
David:	The more we praise God . . . the greater He becomes.
Casey:	And the smaller our problems seem.
Karen:	And then we can understand how He can be in three different places at the same time this Wednesday.
Jerry:	Or save my business.
Lynn:	Or calm my mother and aunt.
David:	I think we just started off wrong tonight. Maybe if everyone is calmed down now . . . we should start all over?
SOUND:	**MUSIC TRANSITION OUT OF DRAMA**
	(Everyone nods in agreement . . . then they close their eyes.)
	Our Father, You are the omnipotent God we love. We praise You, for You are the beginning and ending of all things. Nothing happens without Your knowledge, and we bow before You.
LIGHTS:	**BEGIN FADING DURING PRAYER**
	END

FACING YOUR FEARS

TOPIC
Fear

SYNOPSIS
At Carol's invitation, her fears "show up," thinking that this will be another opportunity to control her with their presence. But this time they are in for a big surprise. It seems Carol has Someone new in her life. She won't be running from her fears anymore.

CAST

Carol – woman who is facing her fears

Fear 1 – one of Carol's fears

Fear 2 – one of Carol's fears

Fear 3 – one of Carol's fears

SETS/PROPS
One platform; three heart-shaped key rings with one key on each; an invitation card.

LIGHTS:	**BLACKOUT** *(Actors move into place)*
SOUND:	**MUSICAL TRANSITION INTO SKETCH AND CONTINUES . . .** **(UNSETTLING, OMINOUS)**
GRAPHIC:	**TITLE SLIDE—** *Facing Your Fears*
LIGHTS:	**UP ON STAGE**

(The stage is dimly lit. The three characters of FEAR stand upstage, on a platform, with their backs to the audience. After a few moments, CAROL walks onstage. As she enters, the light at the center of the stage brightens)

Carol: Hello? I know you're there . . . I can sense you.

(She paces slowly, glancing occasionally around the room)

Look, I know I usually tell you to leave me alone, but this time I want to see you—

Fear 1: *(Turning in the dim light)* —face-to-face. Like your invitation says.

(CAROL reacts to the sound of his voice, but does not turn around to look at him. Her focus remains on the space around her)

Carol: Yes. Face-to-face.

Fear 2: *(Turning around)* Do you have any idea what you're getting into?

Carol: I think so.

Fear 3: *(Turning around)* You shake in your shoes when one of us comes around. I'm dying to see what's going to happen now that all three of us are here.

Fear 1: Carol. *(Takes invitation out of his coat pocket)* Good job on the invitations. We were very excited to receive them.

Fear 2: We thought we should "dress" for the occasion. It's not every day one's worst fears are invited to show up at the same time.

Fear 3: So what's going on, Carol? Why the party?

Carol: I asked you here because I have something very important to tell you.

Fear l: *(Patronizingly)* Oh, an *announcement*.

Fear 2: *(Patronizingly)* Everyone, listen! Carol has mustered up a little courage.

Fear 3: *(Patronizingly)* And we're *dying* to hear what she has to say.

Carol: *(Trying to be courageous)* I want you three out of my life. I'm not afraid of you anymore.

Fear 1: Really.

▸ *Drama Cue: Casting Decision*

When characters represent nonphysical attributes of life (i.e., fear, hate, and love), cast both males and females in the roles. With a gender-specific cast, your audience might mistakenly assume you're making a statement about men or women. A mixed cast will help your audience focus on the attribute, not a gender-specific message.

Fear 2:	*(Patronizingly)* She's not afraid of us anymore.
Fear 3:	Just like that.
Fear 1:	*(Stepping down from the platform and walking menacingly toward her, stopping at CAROL's right. Begins interrogating her)* Tell me, Carol, do you still sleep with a light?
Carol:	*(Somewhat ashamed)* I haven't lately.
Fear 1:	Why do you lock your bedroom door when you live alone in the house?
Carol:	I left it unlocked last night.
Fear 2:	*(Stepping down from the platform and walking to CAROL's left side)* How's the job going, Carol?
Carol:	All right, I guess.
Fear 2:	So tell me, how long are you going to last this time? How long before your boss sees how incompetent you are?
Carol:	*(Trying to be strong)* I'm . . . not . . . incompetent.
Fear 2:	*(Chuckles)* C'mon. *(Begins speaking in a sing-song fashion)* Carol can't do it! She's going to fail again!
Carol:	I'm not listening to you anymore. I'm not afraid.
Fear 3:	*(Stepping down and walking between CAROL and FEAR 2)* But Carol, everyone's afraid of dying. Even you!
Carol:	I'm not so afraid of dying anymore.
Fear 3:	First your grandmother. Then your father. Then your best friend. And who was it recently? Oh yeah, your brother. You could be next, you know.
	(CAROL walks to one side of the stage. FEARS 1–3 line up diagonally from her)
Carol:	Listen, you three have been living in my heart for years. You moved in and basically ruled my life. *(Speaking more boldly)* I am tired of having my fears rule my life! *(Turning her back to the FEARS)* I want the keys to my heart back!
Fear 1:	We've heard that before.
Fear 2:	At least a million times.
Fear 3:	You're not strong enough to take back the keys to your heart.
Carol:	You're right. I've never been successful at overcoming my fears. But something new has happened to me, and I think my life is about to change.
Fear 1:	And what would that be?
Carol:	*(Smiling)* It's not a what. It's a Who.

(The three FEARS are puzzled)

I brought you here to introduce you to Someone new in my life. *(Points upward and out over the audience)* God.

LIGHTS: **DIM LIGHTING NOW IS BROUGHT TO A BRIGHT LIGHT ONSTAGE**

SOUND: **MUSIC STOPS**

(Each FEAR is paralyzed in terror)

Fear 3: *(Frightened)* God.

Carol: God has volunteered to take care of the "fear department" in my life from now on. While I may still be a little uneasy around you, God has promised to take care of you three from here on out.

Fear 2: *(Trying to ease the situation)* Carol, I was only trying to protect you from yourself.

Carol: God's in charge of protecting me now, thank you.

Fear 3: But I'm a reality whether you like it or not.

Carol: True. But I'm no longer afraid of death. You see, I'm never really going to die. I'm God's.

Fear 1: *(Stammering)* We didn't mean you any harm.

Carol: That's funny, because you did a great deal of harm. Now, the keys to my heart, please! *(Puts hand out)*

(Slowly, one by one, each FEAR takes out a heart-shaped key chain with a single key from his coat pocket and places it into CAROL's hand. After they finish, they look up at GOD in fright. CAROL continues.)

(Smiling) So, how does it feel to be afraid?

(The three FEARS look pathetically to her)

(Motioning) Now, get out of my life!

(The three FEARS are motionless for a second, then turn and exit stage . . .)

SOUND: **MUSICAL TRANSITION OUT OF SKETCH AT MOMENT THE THE THREE FEARS TURN TO LEAVE (UPBEAT/VICTORIOUS)**

(CAROL looks at the keys. Then, smiling in victory, she holds the keys up and out before God.)

LIGHTS: **FADE TO BLACK**

END

▸ *Caution: Deliver Yourself from Evil*

Church drama that depicts an aspect of spiritual warfare should be presented tastefully. All too often directors go for the macabre in these situations; when the lights come up, the audience and pastor are left with a sense of oppression. Let the script present the message, not frightening makeup, costumes, SFX, or music.

FEE THYSELF!

TOPIC
Tithing

SYNOPSIS
A self-appointed committee of disgruntled church members are meeting with their pastor in hopes of preventing the pastor's annual stewardship address. They are tired of hearing sermons on the importance of tithing and think they have come up with a better moneymaking system for the church: the Church Fee Program.

SETS/PROPS
A desk, telephone, five chairs, trash can, spiral-bound budget reports, offering place, calculator, large envelope, Styrofoam cups, money, poster board, and five "Church Fee" programs.

CHARACTERS
Pastor Davis – pastor of First Church

Frank – disgruntled tither; complainer, sloppy, abrasive

Wanda – disgruntled tither; prudish, old-fashioned, proper

Hilda – disgruntled tither; strong, decisive, old-fashioned

Jerry – disgruntled tither; pessimistic, cynical

LIGHTS:	**BLACKOUT** *(Actors move into place)*
SOUND:	**MUSICAL TRANSITION INTO SKETCH**
GRAPHIC:	**TITLE SLIDE—** *Fee Thyself!*
LIGHTS:	**UP ON STAGE**

(PASTOR DAVIS sits in his church office talking on the phone. Around his desk are four other chairs and a trash can)

Pastor: *(Speaking into the phone)* Thank you. It was great having you in our church services Sunday and I hope you will visit us again soon. Thank you. You too. Okay, good-bye.

(PASTOR DAVIS walks from behind his desk to the door of his office)

All right. Sorry to keep you all waiting. Won't you come on in?

(FRANK, WANDA, HILDA, and JERRY enter the office. They each carry a spiral-bound budget report in their hands. FRANK carries two reports. They also have Styrofoam cups in their hands. HILDA carries what looks like a poster board covered with a drape. The group looks very solemn and somewhat nervous.)

Pastor: Well, it looks like Jenny took care of you with some of her famous coffee. Won't you sit down, and we can discuss whatever it is you wanted to speak to me about.

(The group sits and no one seems to want to be the first one to speak.)

Okay. Well, apparently you wanted to speak with me about something, so the floor is yours.

(Again, the group looks at each other and around the room, not knowing how to begin.)

Maybe we should begin with a word of prayer?

Frank: *(Blurting out in courage)* Pastor Davis, enough is enough!

Group: Amen!

Pastor: What is enough?

Frank: You know!

Pastor: I don't have the slightest idea what you mean.

Wanda: We are all quite aware of what this Sunday is.

Group: Amen!

Pastor: This Sunday?

▸ *Drama Cue:*
Sit and Deliver

You don't always need elaborate blocking to create a memorable drama. Some of the best sketches call for your cast to simply sit and deliver their lines. Don't incorporate unnecessary moving about the stage if you don't need to.
You'll be surprised how far simple facial expressions and hand gestures can go in making your point.

Hilda:	Your annual stewardship address!
Pastor:	You mean my message on tithing?
Jerry:	Yes, and frankly, Pastor, we feel you're preaching to the choir!
Group:	Amen!
Pastor:	Well, I'm sorry, but part of my responsibility of being the pastor of this church is to teach our people to tithe.
Frank:	*(Patronizing)* We know. Obedience. A tenth. Responsibility.
Wanda:	We've heard it all before.
Hilda:	The practice is old-fashioned and unfair!
Pastor:	It's an act of obedience. And how are we as a church supposed to finance the operation of our church if we don't all tithe?
Jerry:	I'm glad you asked! That's why we're here.
Frank:	Wanda, Hilda, Jerry, and I have come up with a plan to do away with tithing. *(He drops a spiral-bound budget report on the desk in front of the pastor)* Here it is!
Pastor:	What's this?
Frank:	It's a new program to raise money for the church.
Wanda:	It's the Church Fee program.
Pastor:	Church fee?
Hilda:	Instead of tithing, our members will be charged fees.
Group:	Amen!
Pastor:	Fees for what?
Jerry:	For use of the church or its ministries.
Wanda:	Each member pays fees for what he or she personally uses, and nothing more.
Hilda:	Frankly, we are a little tired of funding ministries that don't even benefit us.
Group:	Amen!
Pastor:	I don't understand this at all.
Frank:	Let us show you. Page 1! *(Everyone opens their Church Fee Program reports)* Listed here are the various areas of charges and their corresponding fees.
	(Note: Actors can read fees from Church Fee report. Copy of script should be in report for reference.)
Hilda:	You will see fees for parking in the church parking lot. Some of us walk to church. Pew rental fee. Hymnal fee.

Wanda:	We have created an altar-call toll that must be paid by those who feel the need to go forward during the altar call.
Jerry:	You will pay a monthly retainer fee to have a deacon on call for your household.
Frank:	We also think that people with children should pay for the children's department.
Group:	Amen!
Frank:	So you will see listed a nursery fee, with an additional two dollars if your child will consume graham crackers and juice. We also have a Sunday school Fee. Junior church fee. And the ever-so-needed Crayola fee.
Hilda:	Then there are hospitality fees for the use of Styrofoam cups, creamer, napkins, and Sweet 'n Low!
Jerry:	If your name ever appears on any sort of prayer list, you will be charged a remembered-in-prayer fee.
Wanda:	In a Bible study group? You'll pay a monthly in-the-Word fee!
Frank:	Stand up and give a testimony? You'll pay the sharing fee.
Hilda:	If anyone schedules a meeting with you, Pastor, they will be charged the shepherd's fee.
Pastor:	This doesn't sound at all scriptural!
Frank:	Well, then, you'll be glad to see that we took care of that. You'll notice the John the Baptist fee—that's a fee we've included to cover the cost of baptism.
Wanda:	The Good Samaritan fee is for when you are sick and visited by church staff.
Hilda:	The Samuel fee . . . for baby dedications.
Jerry:	The Lazarus fee . . . for funerals.
Hilda:	We shouldn't have to pay for someone else's passing.
Wanda:	The Upper Room fee will be paid by all who partake in communion. Those plastic cups and wafers aren't cheap!
Group:	Amen!
Pastor:	All I can say is that you have got to be kidding. And how do you intend to take care of the salaries of the church staff?
Frank:	I'm glad you asked. Hilda?
	(During FRANK's following lines, HILDA stands, picks up the poster board, walks over to PASTOR's desk, and unveils the board. It has a hole in it shaped like a head. She puts the board in front of PASTOR, framing him in the poster. On the bottom of the poster hangs a large envelope that says, "I Need You! God Bless.")

CAUTION

▸ *Caution: What a Drag*

Sketches that are "conversationally heavy" can really drag unless you're careful. Keep the tempo quick and energetic, and make sure the actors pick up their cues from line to line—no dead air in between. During your rehearsal, experiment with a line-to-line run-through: have your actors practice delivering their lines as quickly as possible without compromising diction or interpretation. After they've done this a few times, return to your performance tempo. You'll find your actors' pace will be more energetic and punctual.

Each pastor on staff will have his or her picture hung in the front lobby of the church. Each photo will have a money pouch hanging from it. If a church member feels that a particular staff member has blessed them, they put money in that pouch.

Hilda: Why should we take care of a staff member that doesn't affect our lives?

Group: Amen!

Pastor: Whether this is a good idea or not, it is not the scriptural way of giving as God has asked us to give. God has commanded a tenth. It's not my idea; it's God's.

Frank: Look, Pastor. We have prayed about this.

Wanda: In fact, we came thirty minutes early today. We went and sat in the sanctuary. Then, we knelt at the altar to pray over this church fee program.

Jerry: We believe that everyone in our fellowship would be much happier with a giving program like this.

Pastor: So you think you'd like it this way?

Hilda: We would like to *free ourselves* from the archaic practice of tithing.

Group: Amen!

Pastor: *(Sitting in silence for a moment)* Well . . . I guess we could try this. When did you want to begin?

Jerry: As soon as possible.

Pastor: *(Toying with them)* For the record, I am totally against this. As your pastor I feel I answer to God before I answer to you, but I guess we could try it.

Frank: *(Standing)* We hoped you'd see it our way. *(To the group)* Let's go.

(The group stands and begins ad-libbing their good-byes when . . .)

Pastor: Oh, before you go, we need to settle up.

Wanda: Settle up?

Pastor: Yes. *(Pulls the church fee program and a calculator to him)*

Frank: What's going on here?

Pastor: If we are going to start on this new stewardship plan, then there is no better time than the present.

(Group sits in bewilderment. PASTOR starts clicking keys on the calculator, calculating each fee as he goes. He is positive and upbeat.)

(Note: Pastor can pretend to be looking for fees on the report but can actually read the following:)

So let's see here. You each used the parking lot. You said you sat in the sanctuary pews. And apparently you went to the altar to pray, which would fall under the altar toll. I see that you helped yourself to coffee, so we'll need to include the hospitality fee. You met with me, the pastor, so that's twenty-five-dollar shepherd's fee right there. And you each shared, so there's that sharing fee.

Frank: Uh, just a minute, there, Pastor . . .

Pastor: Let's see here . . . the total comes to . . . divided by the four of you . . . Okay, for today's visit, you each owe sixty-one dollars and forty-three cents! Amen?

(PASTOR pulls an offering plate from under the desk and hands it to FRANK)

SOUND: **MUSICAL TRANSITION OUT OF SKETCH**

(The stunned group sits in bewilderment, taken completely by surprise. They look at each, other not knowing what to do. The group slowly passes their church fee programs to FRANK. FRANK takes the pastor's report, then throws them all in the trash can. The group begins to exit)

Pastor: So, I'll see you all this Stewardship Sunday?

(The group nods their heads . . . and turn to go)

Hilda: Dumb idea, Frank!

Frank: It wasn't my idea, it was Jerry's!

Jerry: No, it wasn't!

Wanda: Nice try, Frank . . .

(Group ad-libs bickering as they exit)

LIGHTS: **FADE TO BLACK**

END

BACK TO SQUARE ONE

TOPIC
Sin/danger of falling back into the same sin after you thought you learned your lesson.

SYNOPSIS
Tony returns to "square one," where he finds the familiar faces of those who can't achieve victory over sin. Each person claims to have learned his lesson but ultimately ends up back where he started. While Tony isn't ready to let his mistake stop him from trying again, the others have given up in defeat and made "square one" their home.

CHACTERS
Lola – "square one" inhabitant

Charlie – "square one" inhabitant

Morris – "square one" inhabitant

Mandy – "square one" inhabitant

Tony – returning to "square one"

SETS/PROPS
No specific set is required, but if you can perform this sketch on a platform set in the shape of a square, that will add to the "square one" theme. Each character requires specific props: *LOLA* needs a magazine, a pillow, and a can of soda; *CHARLIE* should be sitting in a lawn chair and have a television remote in his hand; *MORRIS* has his cell phone and briefcase with him; and *MANDY* is sitting in a lawn chair doing needlepoint or knitting.

LIGHTS:	**BLACKOUT** *(Actors move into place)*
SOUND:	**MUSICAL TRANSITION INTO SKETCH**
GRAPHIC:	**TITLE SLIDE—** *Back to Square One*
LIGHTS:	**UP ON STAGE**

(There are four people sitting in "square one." Square one is the place you return when you've fallen back into the sin you thought you were set free from. For being in such a defeating place, LOLA, CHARLIE, MANDY, and MORRIS seem quite content. LOLA sits on the side of square one next to her pillow, lazily reading a magazine and sipping her soda. CHARLIE sits in a lawn chair, remote in hand, watching an imaginary television and reacting to whatever he is "seeing." MANDY also sits in a lawn chair, happily doing needlepoint or knitting. MORRIS is upstage, pacing and pantomiming a conversation on his cell phone.)

Lola: *(Without looking up from her magazine)* What time is it?

Charlie: What?

Lola: *(Loudly)* I said, what time is it?

Morris: *(Covering the phone)* Shh! This is a very important call!

Lola: Then take it somewhere else!

(LOLA, CHARLIE and MANDY all look at each other and laugh.)

Mandy: Like that would ever happen! And to answer your question, Lola, it's 4:30 in the afternoon.

Lola: So I guess it is too late for us to try to do anything today.

Charlie: Suppose so.

Mandy: Besides, I'm kinda liking it here.

Lola: Me too. At first I just wanted to go! You know, get moving. But I'm not so sure now.

Charlie: This place grows on you, doesn't it?

Mandy: Sure does.

(A very defeated TONY enters. He is a mixed bag of sadness, anger, humiliation, and frustration. He stops just short of "square one.")

Lola: Well, well, well, well, well! Look who's back!

Charlie: Tony.

Mandy: Back so soon?

(TONY just stands there hanging his head)

▸ *Drama Cue:*
Keep it Real

This drama calls for real people! Now is not the time to create out-of-the-box characters in an attempt to get a laugh. Each of these characters represents people sitting in your congregation—relate to them by helping them identify with one of these everyday characters.

Tony:	Hello, everybody.
Lola:	Well, come on in, there's plenty of room.
Charlie:	Find you a place to park. You know the drill.
Mandy:	Sorry, but I'm not giving back your chair. You left and said you were never coming back.
Lola:	We all said we were never coming back to "square one."
Tony:	But I really thought I learned my lesson.
	(MORRIS gets off the phone.)
Morris:	Hey, I was on an important business call. Can't you hold it down?
Lola:	Your business practices are what are keeping you here, Morris.
Morris:	*(Sees TONY)* Tony? Back so soon?
	(TONY walks up on the platform and stands CS.)
Charlie:	I hate to be the one to say it, but I told you so!
Lola:	Me too!
Mandy:	Me too!
Morris:	Me too!
Tony:	I know, I know. But I confessed my sin, asked God to forgive me, and it was time to move on.
Lola:	Been there. Done that!
Tony:	But I really thought that this time . . .
Mandy:	That this time things were going to be different, right?
Tony:	Right.
Mandy:	Did you read your Bible?
Tony:	Occasionally.
Charlie:	Pray?
Tony:	Not very often.
Morris:	Stay in church?
Tony:	Not really.
Mandy:	Start doing things that caused you to fall before?
Tony:	Yes.
Mandy:	And then?
Tony:	I messed up.

Lola:	*(Very theatrically)* So welcome back to "square one"!
Tony:	But I don't want to be here.
Morris:	You should've thought of that before you sinned.
Mandy:	Should've, would've, could've! It's all so complicated. It's so much easier not to fight it.
Lola:	I hear you, sister!
Tony:	What do you mean? Just stay here at "square one" and quit trying to live a godly life?
Mandy:	Yep!
Charlie:	Now you're talking!
Morris:	Amen!
Lola:	That's what we're doing.
Tony:	But God doesn't want us to live a complacent life. He wants us to confess our sin, forsake it, and move on.
Lola:	Appears to me you didn't do a very good job forsaking it.
Tony:	Yeah, you're right. I guess I wasn't walking in the power of the Holy Spirit. I tried to live a righteous life in my own strength.
Lola:	Like that will ever work. *(Picks up her pillow and tosses it to TONY)* Take this. You might as well stay here at "square one" with us, and get some rest.
Morris:	Quit fighting it.
Charlie:	And forget about it.
Mandy:	Kick back, like we're doing.
Lola:	Living here at "square one" isn't that bad. Right, gang?
SOUND:	**MUSICAL TRANSITION OUT OF SKETCH**
	(TONY slowly looks at each of the others. He drops his head momentarily and then looks upward.)
Tony:	Father, forgive me of my sin. I thought I learned my lesson, but I didn't. I see how I walked right back down the path of my old ways. But I don't want to stay here at "square one," defeated and complacent. So if You will forgive me, through the Holy Spirit's power it's time to move on.
	(TONY ends his prayer. Giving the pillow back to LOLA, he moves to the edge of the platform and turns around to face the others. Those who have been cynical up to this point, now have a look of admiration on their faces. For a fleeting moment they wish they had the strength to do what TONY is doing.)
	Anyone want to go with me? You want to quit living back here at "square one"?

CAUTION

▸ *Caution: Open Space*

An open stage is an open space for the imagination. If a sketch does not call for a specific place but an imaginary place, keep the stage free of distracting scenery. Let the characters and the situation create the place in the minds of your audience.

(The others hold his gaze for a brief moment. Then MORRIS turns and begins to dial on his cell phone. MANDY looks down and continues to do her crafting. CHARLIE looks away from TONY and starts watching his imaginary television program once again.)

Lola: *(Humbly)* See you soon?

Tony: By the grace of God, I'm never coming back to "square one."

Lola: *(Tenderly)* God bless you, Tony. Good-bye.

Tony: Good-bye.

(TONY turns and exits. MORRIS, CHARLIE, and MANDY are still doing what they did at the beginning of the sketch, but LOLA doesn't return immediately to her magazine. Instead, she stares somberly out toward the audience, thinking about where she is living.)

LIGHTS: FADE TO BLACK

END

BACK TROUBLE

TOPIC

Spending too much time looking back at a church's accomplishments
can hinder a congregation from looking forward to the continuing
work of Jesus Christ.

SYNOPSIS

A local church congregation looks back upon all their accomplishments.
They have carried out the Great Commission in many ways. They are
satisfied with what they've done in the past until they turn around and see
the kingdom work that still needs doing.

SETS/PROPS

A mini-church is set up onstage. Four to five chairs sit in a row facing the
front. A small podium (or pulpit) should be at CS. Actors should hold white
Styrofoam coffee cups in their hands.

CHARACTERS

Leland – witness

Sarah – prayer warrior

Pastor – pastor

Carol – counselor

Bonnie – Sunday school teacher

Little child – Nonspeaking

Street person – Nonspeaking

Church member – Nonspeaking

LIGHTS:	**BLACKOUT** *(Actors move into place)*
SOUND:	**MUSIC TRANSITION INTO SKETCH**
GRAPHIC:	**TITLE SLIDE—** *Back Trouble*
LIGHTS:	**UP ON STAGE**

(We see a stage set to look like the inside of a church sanctuary. Chairs or small church pews face the audience. A small pulpit is off to one side. LELAND, SARAH, PASTOR, CAROL, and BONNIE are standing or sitting with their backs to the audience, looking out behind the pews as if they are surveying all their accomplishments.)

▸ *Drama Cue: Transitional Music*

Transitional music can help introduce an emotional change for your audience. In this drama, music plays a key role in helping the congregation transition from past accomplishments to a hope-filled future. Use music that represents feelings of optimism and accomplishment.

Leland: Wow . . . look at it. Amazing!

Sarah: Who would have thought we could accomplish all this?

Pastor: Well, that's why I called this little celebration today. I wanted a chance to tell you what a great congregation you are!

Carol: I don't want to sound prideful, but . . . we really know how to do this church stuff, don't we?

Bonnie: I'd say we have it down pretty good!

Leland: Yeah, you might say we've mastered the old church program!

Carol: We could write the how-to book for church congregations!

Pastor: You've all put a lot of prayer, time, and effort into making our church the role model for other congregations.

Bonnie: Like our Sunday school program . . . it's the best! Looking back, I can't believe all the children we've taught over the years. I'm overwhelmed by how much has been done!

Pastor: Job well done, Bonnie.

Carol: And just look at the hundreds of people we have counseled and encouraged. Being a part of the counseling ministry has really been fulfilling to me.

Sarah: As I look back, I see the results of hours upon hours of prayer . . . including the calluses on my knees. I'm a believer that prayer changes things . . . just look!

Leland: This was a great idea. Taking the time to stop and look back on all our accomplishments is exciting. I see the faces of all the men and women we witnessed to that came to know the Lord. But I've got to tell you something.

Pastor: What's that?

Leland: *(With a slight chuckle)* I'm tired. It's been work.

Sarah: Sure it has. But most of the hard work is over. Just look at how many people in our community we've reached for Christ!

Carol: There aren't too many more people in our scope of influence.

Bonnie:	Besides, it's okay to slow down a bit and give some of the other churches a chance to catch up with us.
Leland:	I agree. We've done our part. Let someone else do it now. Frankly, I like stopping to remember the "good old days."
Sarah:	Me too. I could sit here forever!
Pastor:	We sure have had some wonderful years. We are comfortably blessed. I found a verse about that. Let me grab my Bible.
	(PASTOR finally turns toward the audience and crosses to where his Bible is lying on a chair. As he picks up his Bible . . .)
SOUND:	**BACKGROUND MUSIC THAT CONTINUES THROUGH END OF SKETCH.**
	(When the music starts, PASTOR reacts as if he hears the voices of the souls in his community he hasn't reached. He then turns towards the audience . . . and is awestruck as he appears to now see all the work that still needs to be done. He lingers. The others turn to see what's keeping PASTOR. Then, one by one, they see what PASTOR is seeing. Finally, they are all lined up onstage.)
Pastor:	Just look.
Leland:	More. There are more who need Christ.
Sarah:	I thought we had done all we possibly could.
Bonnie:	Look at all the children. Who will care for them?
Carol:	And I had no idea we still had so many hurting in the congregation.
Leland:	So many . . . why didn't we see them?
Pastor:	Because we have back trouble. We continue to relish the accomplishments that are behind us . . .
Leland:	. . . instead of anticipating the great things God has for us in the future.
Sarah:	I see now. We've done a lot, but there is much more to do.
Carol:	And we'll never meet the needs of others if we continue to turn our backs on them.
Pastor:	That's right. If we're going to have back trouble in this church, it's going to be the backbreaking work of ministry. Do we all agree? Let's get busy.
	(They now move to different parts of the stage as each prepares to get down to business. LELAND removes his jacket and begins rolling up his shirtsleeves. SARAH moves to a pew, takes what looks like a prayer list from her purse, kneels, and begins praying. CAROL retrieves her Bible, takes off some of her fancy jewelry, and sits to one side. BONNIE slips on some tennis shoes and then removes a children's book and Bible from her bag. The PASTOR moves to the podium and begins praying.)

▸ *Caution:*
A Little Extra Work

There is a period of time in this drama when the audience will not see the actors' faces. You want to hold your audience's attention, so you may have to do a little extra work with your actors' movements and gestures to keep your congregation engaged.

(The LITTLE CHILD then enters and goes to BONNIE, who greets him/her with a hug. They sit down together as she begins to pantomime teaching a Bible story. LELAND moves downstage, a New Testament and gospel tracts in his hand. At this point a CHURCH MEMBER make his/her way to the platform . . . in tears . . . and goes to CAROL for help. They hug, and then CAROL begins counseling the CHURCH MEMBER. At this point, the STREET PERSON passes by LELAND. LELAND hands him a tract and invites him to sit and talk about Christ's love. The two sit. The PASTOR moves the small podium to CS. He opens his Bible, and then slowly lifts his head upward. At this point, the church members all stand and look upward, in a show of obedience.)

LIGHTS: **FADE TO BLACK**

                  END

The Befores and After

TOPIC
Saved by grace: Examining the before and after of a life saved by grace.

SCRIPTURE
Ephesians 2:1-10

SYNOPSIS
The Befores are dead in their trespasses of sin. They spend their lives fulfilling the desires of the flesh and mind, and have lifted themselves to goodness by works. When After passes their way, the Befores taunt and tease him because he is no longer a part of their group. The difference between the Befores and After is that After has been saved by grace. It is not his works that have lifted him up, but the gift of God through Jesus Christ the Lord.

CAST
Before 1 – unsaved, dead in trespasses of sin

Before 2 – unsaved, dead in trespasses of sin

Before 3 – unsaved, dead in trespasses of sin

Before 4 – unsaved, dead in trespasses of sin

After – saved by grace

SETS/PROPS
No specific set is needed. Props: five stools.

LIGHTS:	**BLACKOUT** *(Actors move into place)*
SOUND:	**MUSICAL TRANSITION INTO SKETCH**
GRAPHIC:	**TITLE SLIDE—** *The Befores and After*
LIGHTS:	**UP ON STAGE**

(We see BEFORE 1, 2, 3, and 4 on stage, sitting on stools across CS. The BEFORES look a little rough, edgy, and harsh. They are talking about their weekend . . .)

Before 1: So guys, what's it going to be this weekend?

Before 2: I've barely recovered from last weekend!

Before 3: I've lived this whole week like it's my last weekend on earth, if you know what I mean!

(The BEFORES laugh . . .)

Before 4: Look, I don't know about you boys, but I am ready to tear it up!

Before 1: Me too! I just want to go where I want!

Before 2: Do what I want!

Before 3: Say what I want!

Before 4: Think what I want!

Before 1: And not feel guilty about it the next day, right?

All: Right!

Before 2: Let's break all the rules!

Before 3: *(Playing dumb)* Rules? What are rules?

Before 4: No one tells us how to live, isn't that right, boys?

All: That's right!

Before 1: You know what I find too good?

Before 2: What's that?

Before 1: Being bad!

Before 3: No, bad is better than good. It's great!

Before 4: We're great!

(Guys agree. AFTER enters . . . walks by the BEFORES.)

Before 1: Oh, look here! Who's this? He looks a little familiar, don't he, guys?

(AFTER stops . . . knowing that he is ready to get razzed by the BEFORES.)

▸ *Drama Cue:*
Color Me Different

When you want to distinguish between two types of people in a drama, use color. In this sketch, for example, dress the Befores in dark colors and have your After wear white or brightly colored clothing. Little touches of color and the way a character's costume is worn can help your audience distinguish between good and evil.

Before 2:	Oh, yeah, I know that face. He used to be one of us!
Before 3:	Hey, After.
After:	Hello, Befores.
Before 4:	So After, what are you doing in these parts? What would people say if they saw you with your old gang?
Before 1:	You miss hanging out with us?
After:	Those days are over. I'm much happier now.
Before 2:	Now that you are *better* than us, right?
After:	I'm not better than you, I've just found grace.
Before 3:	Oh that's right, grace. *(Sarcastic)* Grace has cleaned you all up!
After:	Grace has raised me up.
Before 4:	Look at us! We're raised up!
Before 1:	We're pretty high up here! I'd say we're raised up a lot higher than you are, pal!
After:	*You've* raised yourselves up! God didn't.
Before 2:	And that don't count?
Before 3:	We spent a lot of time working hard to get up here where we are!
After:	But look at your foundation? *(Referring to the stools)* It can be knocked out from underneath you at any time. God's grace grounds you on a firm foundation.
Before 4:	So just what are you saying, After?
Before 1:	He's saying we're not good enough for God! And I say that's not true. Sure, we don't live perfect lives most of the time. But we do a lot of things to make up for it!
Before 2:	We're kind to people!
Before 3:	We give to the poor!
Before 4:	We even go to church now and then!
Before 1:	We do good to work off the bad!
After:	Your good works will never be good enough.
	(There is silence for a moment. Then . . .)
Before 4:	Is that why we're Befores . . . and you're an After?
After:	*(Nodding his head and speaking softly)* Yes. And every time I think about it, I'm amazed. I couldn't do anything to deserve it, but He shows His grace to me. His grace is there for you if you want it.
	(The BEFORES slowly drop their heads one at a time . . .)

▸ *Caution:*
Can't Place 'Em

So you want to create some bad guys? When in a comedy setting, use accents or mannerisms associated with a negative social element to get your point across. But when performing a serious drama with an important message like this one, veer clear of accents and stereotypes. If your audience can place the "bad guys," the sketch becomes an observation on people from that segment of society and could be potentially offensive.

SOUND: "YOUR GRACE STILL AMAZES ME" –
             BY PHILLIPS, CRAIG & DEAN

             (Last chorus ... bridge ... final chorus 2:50)

             *(After song begins, AFTER walks upstage toward the audience .
             .. looks up to heaven ... then kneels and bows his head. During
             the bridge of the song, one at a time, the BEFORES raise their
             heads to see AFTER. Then during the final chorus, each of the
             BEFORES, again one at a time, come down off their stools,
             walk forward and kneel next to AFTER. Now in an attitude of
             prayer, they have all become AFTERS.)*

LIGHTS: FADE TO BLACK

             END

A Matter of Seconds

TOPIC
Our heavenly Father is a God of second chances.

SCRIPTURE
Jonah 2

SYNOPSIS
A young man regrets his disobedience to his father. He wonders if there is any chance that his father will forgive him and let him try again. After receiving grim advice from the Discouragers, the man's father shows up and, in true form fatherly fashion, forgives his son . . . and is willing to give him a second chance.

SETS/PROPS
The only furniture needed is a chair sitting center stage. Props: Son should have a backpack.

CHARACTERS
Son – has been disobedient to his father

Discourager 1 – sarcastic, caustic

Discourager 2 – blunt, hard

Father – a father of second chances

LIGHTS:	**BLACKOUT** *(Actors move into place)*
SOUND:	**MUSIC TRANSITION INTO SKETCH**
GRAPHIC:	**TITLE SLIDE—** *A Matter of Seconds*
LIGHTS:	**LIGHTS UP—STAGE IS LIT DIMLY WITH MORE LIGHT JUST AROUND WHERE THE SON SITS. IT IS OKAY TO HAVE THE DISCOURAGERS "LIVE IN THE SHADOWS" AND ON OCCASION STAND OR MOVE INTO THE BRIGHTER LIGHT.**

(SON sits alone, his head in his hands. His backpack sits next to the chair. DISCOURAGER 1 and DISCOURAGER 2 enter, and stop together in the shadows.)

Disc 1: *(Sarcastic . . . cynical)* Ah . . . now what do we have here? Someone's sitting in the chair . . . he's got his bags packed. I wonder what has happened.

Son: *(Looking up from his hands. He seems beaten)* Leave me alone.

Disc 1: Hmm . . . he doesn't sound very good either. I bet I know what's going on.

Son: Please . . .

Disc 2: *(Speaking bluntly, with no emotion)* You blew it. Right?

Son: *(Again, slowly looks up and over to DISCOURAGER 2, then speaks with obvious pain . . .)* Yeah. I can't believe it. Why did I do it? I love him.

Disc 2: Love who?

Son: *(Sorrowfully)* My father.

Disc 1: Ow! *(With a smile, not even realizing the kid's pain)* You know how to pick 'em! What were you thinking? Kid, you're in big trouble.

(SON puts his face back into his hands. The two DISCOURAGERS look at one another . . .)

Disc 2: So, what are you going to do now?

Son: I don't know . . . maybe my father will give me a second chance?

Disc 1: Fat chance of that. As I recall, you've been in this same place before. Right?

(SON nods his head)

(Laughs to himself) Boy, you've already had your chance. Disobeying your father is a pretty big offense, especially when you're a repeat offender.

Son: But maybe if I go to him . . . ask his forgiveness . . . maybe he'd give me a break? Maybe I could . . .

▶ *Drama Cue:*
 Keep it Cool

There is nothing more powerful than a parable drama. When an earthly drama has heavenly meaning the audience really connects with it, so keep this drama real by making the son and father everyday characters. This way the audience won't have to sort through a clutter of costumes, hairstyles, and makeup. Remember, a simplified approach is stronger than an overly produced sketch.

Disc 1:	Maybe, maybe, maybe . . . would've, could've, should've. It's too late! What's done is done.
Son:	I know, but I really am sorry!
Disc 2:	You've been sorry before. How many times is your father supposed to hear "I'm sorry" before he is completely disgusted with you? Huh?
	(SON lowers head once more.)
	I hate to be the one to tell you, but it just doesn't work that way.
Son:	Then what am I going to do now?
Disc 1:	*(Flippantly)* You're on your own . . . big deal! You're too old to be worried about meeting your father's approval.
Disc 2:	You need to grow up.
	(The last line sobers SON somewhat.)
Son:	But I want to do what my father wants me to do.
Disc 1:	*(Waving him off)* You're hopeless.
	(DISC 1 kneels into the light, right next to SON)
Disc 2:	*(Slowly, manipulatively)* Look, we know who your father is. And while he's a good guy and all, he's not *that* good.
Disc 1:	*(Kneeling down on the other side of SON)* And apparently . . . you aren't all that good, either.
Disc 2:	Are you really deserving of another chance?
Son:	I won't do it again.
Disc 2:	Look at me. Are you going to sit there and tell me that you'll never disobey your father again? That you'll never make another mistake?
Son:	*(Thinks for a moment . . . then speaks with painful honesty)* No . . . I can't tell you that.
Disc 2:	Then c'mon, grab your stuff, let's go.
Disc 1:	Yeah. Let's get out of here. No use you sitting here wallowing in regret.
	(SON stands. Then in the darkness, from the front of auditorium . . .)
Father:	Not so fast.
Son:	*(Looking out)* Father?
	(FATHER now walks into the stage area with the others)
LIGHTS:	SOMEWHAT BRIGHTER ON STAGE AS FATHER SETS FOOT ON STAGE

> ▸ *Caution: Sidetracked*

It is easy to be sidetracked with a drama like this. Don't make the mistake of focusing too much on the "dark" side of this sketch. Make everything about the reconciliation of the father and son. Don't make the mistake of getting so caught up in the dramatic peril that the drama can't rise above it. It is the hope that you want to focus on . . . use your attention to detail there!

Father: Son.

Son: Father, I'm so sorry. I didn't know what to do.

Disc 1: Forget it, kid . . . your father doesn't want to hear your lame excuses.

Son: But . . .

Disc 2: Have some self-respect! Don't beg for his mercy . . .

Father: Enough! You two may leave.

Disc 2: He's ours . . .

Father: He's mine and he will always be mine. Now leave!

SOUND: **TRANSITION MUSIC OUT OF SKETCH**

(DISC 1 looks a little shaken . . . begins to exit. DISC 2 stands glaring, staring down at the father in hatred. He slowly brings his arm up and points at the father as if to say something, then turns and leaves. FATHER crosses over to the SON. They look at each other for a moment. Finally . . .)

Son: *(Broken)* Father, please forgive me.

Father: *(After a moment, smiles)* You're forgiven. Son, why did you run?

Son: Because I messed up again. But, if you'll only give me another chance . . . a second chance . . .

(FATHER doesn't let him finish. He hugs SON. MUSIC SWELLS. They embrace for a moment. Afterward . . .)

Father: Let's go home, Son.

(SON smiles, picks up his bag. The FATHER motions that he'll carry it for him. Together they exit into the darkness.)

LIGHTS: **LIGHTS FADE TO BLACK**

END

MR. RIGHT

TOPIC

When you are in God's will, He will arrange for the right person,
in the right place, and at the right time.

SCRIPTURE

Ruth 2:11-23

SYNOPSIS

Six people are trapped in an elevator . . . good thing Mr. Right is on board.
Knowing that God puts him in the right place at the right time,
Mr. Right is cool, calm, and collected while the others are frantic or upset.
During their close encounter, Mr. Right acknowledges that he is
a Christian, which fascinates the others . . . they've all been wanting to
know more about God.

SETS/PROPS

No set is required. However, you may want to place tape on the stage
or use a three-sided set to replicate an elevator. Characters use hand
props as suggested throughout the script.

CAST

Agnes – inconvenienced

Stuart – nervous

Oswald – claustrophobic

Paula – frantic

Torrey – fidgety

Mr. Right – Christian; cool, calm

LIGHTS:	**BLACKOUT** *(Actors move into place)*
SOUND:	**MUSICAL TRANSITION INTO SKETCH**
GRAPHIC:	**TITLE SLIDE—** *Mr. Right*
LIGHTS:	**UP ON STAGE**

(For only a moment we see a bare stage. Then the cast begins to arrive at the elevator ... PAULA runs in and moves to the elevator and quickly punches the button ... in fact, she punches it a few times; she is in a hurry. STUART, carrying a briefcase, enters and walks to the elevator ... punches the button. AGNES enters ... pushes her way past STUART and punches the button ...)

Paula: *(Who has been annoyed by the last two button pushers ...)* When the light is on, it means that someone already pushed the button and called for the elevator. You don't need to push it again!

Agnes: *(Giving PAULA the evil eye)* You never can be too sure, honey.

(TORREY enters. She is carrying a big purse and a lunch bag of some sort. She has an iPod on and is listening to music. She moves to the elevator and punches the button. This gets a big sigh from PAULA. Then OSWALD enters. He appears to be very scared ... he stops before he reaches the elevator ... and very nervously he moves toward the button.)

Paula: Sir, the button has already been pushed!

Oswald: I know ... but I have to push it for myself.

(OSWALD pushes the button. MR. RIGHT then enters. He is dressed in a suit. He carries a briefcase ... He moves to the elevator ... but doesn't push the button. PAULA is impressed. Finally ...)

SOUND: **ELEVATOR DOOR OPENING**

(The group proceeds to step inside the elevator ... PAULA enters and hits the button for the floor she wants. AGNES reaches over and hits a button. STUART enters ...)

Paula: Floor?

Stuart: Thirty-two, please.

Torrey: *(Entering)* Twenty-eight. Thank you!

Mr. Right: Thirty, please. Thank you.

(OSWALD moves to the buttons ...)

Paula: Floor?

Oswald: I have to push the button myself. It's part of my therapy. *(Pushes the button, then nervously runs to the back of the elevator and holds on.)*

SOUND:	ELEVATOR DOOR SHUTS; ELEVATOR MUSIC BEGINS PLAYING

(The group exhibits the discomfort that comes with being in a crowded elevator with a group of strangers. They steal looks at one another ... then ...)

SOUND:	MUSIC WINDS TO A STOP

(Everyone in the elevator jerks, as if the elevator has suddenly stopped)

Agnes: We've stopped!

Stuart: Oh, my goodness!

Paula: I can't believe it!

Oswald: We're all going to die!

Torrey: Bummer!

Oswald: I knew this was going to happen!

Agnes: I wonder what's wrong. I hope the building is not on fire.

Stuart: Fire?

Agnes: Maybe there has been a power outage.

Oswald: No power?

Agnes: Maybe the old elevator cable is just worn out! You know, it's scary to think that the builders of this building probably went with the lowest bidder to install this elevator.

Oswald: Oh no!

Paula: *(To AGNES)* Would you stop it! You're scaring everybody. There's an emergency phone right here. I'll find out what's going on. *(She picks up an imaginary phone from the wall ...)* Hello? Hello? We're stuck in the elevator ...

Torrey: What are they saying?

Paula: Nothing. The phone's deader than a doornail! *(Hanging up)* Great—now I'm late for my job interview!

Stuart: I've got an important business meeting. *(Begins to pace in the elevator)*

Oswald: I finally get up enough courage to take an elevator and this is what happens.

Agnes: Courage? Courage for what?

Oswald: I'm claustrophobic. My therapist suggested I do this. It's taken me a year of therapy to get up the nerve!

Torrey: Well, it looks like we're going to be here for a while.

(She takes a sandwich out of her bag and is ready to eat it when ...)

▶ *Drama Cue: Character Is King*

This drama just cries out for some fun characters. So create them! Begin by working with the actors on their characterizations, and then add creative costuming and accessories. But remember, don't let your actors' lines get buried in their characterization. Message first!

Paula:	For heaven's sake, what is that smell? What are you eating?
Torrey:	It's just an egg salad sandwich.
Agnes:	We're in an elevator here! Please!
Oswald:	I'm allergic to eggs.
Torrey:	Whatever. *(She puts the sandwich away)*
Paula:	*(To STUART)* And would you stop pacing!
Agnes:	This day has been nothing but trouble!
Paula:	Where were you going?
Agnes:	Up to do some volunteer work for the Red Cross.
Torrey:	Oh, that's where I'm going, too. It looks like we'll be volunteering together.
Agnes:	Oh, great!
Oswald:	So now what do we do?
Paula:	We just wait. What else can we do? We're suspended between heaven and earth in this elevator shaft.
Agnes:	We could fall to our death any minute!
	(OSWALD cringes . . . everyone but MR. RIGHT gives AGNES a dirty look)
	Oops! Sorry.
Paula:	*(To MR. RIGHT)* You sure are calm. You haven't said a word.
Stuart:	Yeah! How can you remain so calm at a time like this?
Mr. Right:	I've come to believe that nothing is an accident.
Torrey:	Huh?
Mr. Right:	I believe there is a reason for all of this. It will be interesting to see what happens.
Agnes:	So where did you learn foolishness like that, some self-help course?
Mr. Right:	Actually, from the Bible.
Stuart:	Are you a Christian?
Mr. Right:	Yes.
Oswald:	You're not a priest or a minister or anything like that, are you?
Mr. Right:	No. I just feel that God places me where I should be for a particular purpose.
Agnes:	Well, unless you know how to restart this elevator, I can't see your purpose here.

> ▸ *Caution: Opposites Attract*

When your have an opposite character like Mr. Right, leave him alone. Your audience will recognize the contrast of Mr. Right compared to the rest of the characters in the elevator. Keeping him simple will make him much more attractive to your audience.

Paula:	Actually, I was listening to Christian radio for the first time the other day. I have a lot of questions . . . I wanted to find someone who could give me some answers . . .
Stuart:	You know, I just started reading the Bible. But there's a lot I don't understand.
Mr. Right:	I'd be glad to answer any questions you might have.
Torrey:	*(Spraying cologne . . . causing the others to cringe)* I used to go to church as a girl . . . but I've drifted away. Do you know of a good church I could go to?
Oswald:	I've tried therapy. Maybe I need to give God a chance!
	(The whole elevator looks at AGNES)
Agnes:	All right1 I admit it! I'm a little rough around the edges. I need a change too!
Mr. Right:	Wow. Look what's happened here. Do you think it was by chance we all entered this elevator . . . that we got stuck in here together . . . that I am a Christian . . . and that all of you having been looking for spiritual answers?
Paula:	That would be quite a coincidence.
Agnes:	Listen, I find it hard to believe that we're stuck here on purpose. So what now, the elevator is going to start because we found "Mr. Right"?
SOUND:	**MUZAK RESTARTS**
	(Everyone jerks, letting us know the elevator is moving again)
Oswald:	We're moving again!
	(Everyone stares at MR. RIGHT as if he is some kind of angel.)
Paula:	*(To MR. RIGHT)* I don't want to intrude, but after we get off this elevator, can I ask you a few questions?
Mr. Right:	Sure, but what about your job interview?
Paula:	That can wait. Like you said . . . you are here for a reason, and I think that reason is me!
SOUND:	**DOOR OPENS**
Stuart:	I think I'm a reason, too. Can I join you?
Oswald:	I want to come!
Torrey:	Don't leave me out!
Agnes:	You've already made a believer out of me! Count me in, too!
Mr. Right:	But this isn't your floor. This is the restaurant level.
Paula:	Then we can stop for lunch and have our questions answered by Mr. Right.

Mr. Right:	Mr. Right?
Agnes:	You were the right person, in the right place, at the right time!
All:	Mr. Right.
SOUND:	**MUSICAL TRANSITION OUT OF SKETCH**
Mr. Right:	All right, let's go!
	(Group ad-libs their comments as they exit the elevator . . .)
Torrey:	I hope the restaurant has egg salad!
LIGHTS:	**FADE TO BLACK**
	END

MYSTERIOUS

TOPIC
Marriage: Submission and respect

SCRIPTURE
Ephesians 5:22-33

SYNOPSIS
Jaden and Sandra are returning and recovering from a family reunion. While sitting in the airport, they begin to talk about all of the dysfunctional marriages in their family. Soon they start questioning the way their own marriages are working. They are caught off guard when a couple of strangers offer some uninvited marriage counseling. The whole thing is *mysterious!*

CHARACTERS

Jaden – 30s; husband to Sandra

Sandra – 30s; wife to Jaden

Ben – traveler

Linda – traveler

SETS/PROPS
Sketch takes place in the terminal of an airport. Props: eight chairs, carry-on luggage, and two magazines.

LIGHTS:	**BLACKOUT** *(Actors move into place)*
SOUND:	**MUSICAL TRANSITION INTO SKETCH**
GRAPHIC:	**TITLE SLIDE—** *Mysterious*
LIGHTS:	**UP ON STAGE**

(We see JADEN and SANDRA sitting in the terminal of an airport. They sit in the middle two chairs in a row of four chairs. An identical row is behind them facing the other way, the backs of the chairs touching—like you would see in an airport. BEN sits with his back to us on the back row, end chair SR. LINDA sits with her back to us on the back row, end chair SL. Each person has a carry-on by their feet.)

Jaden: *(Thumbing through a magazine)* How much longer until our flight leaves?

Sandra: *(Thumbing through a magazine)* For the fourth time, we board in fifteen minutes. Are you anxious to get home, or what!

Jaden: You have no idea.

Sandra: I forgot how much you hated our family reunions.

Jaden: You have no idea.

Sandra: It was good to see both of our families.

Jaden: Good that we won't have to go through another reunion for two more years.

Sandra: It will take us that long to get ready for the next one.

Jaden: Sandra, I want to say something, and I don't want you to get offended.

Sandra: Okay.

Jaden: Your family is weird!

Sandra: My family? What about yours?

Jaden: Weird as well! Can you believe how my dad bosses my mom around?

Sandra: At least they didn't scream at each other like my parents were constantly doing.

Jaden: And what's up with Uncle Ralph and Aunt Ida?

Sandra: They can barely stand to be in the same room. Not like my sister and brother-in-law.

Jaden: Could they be any more fake!

Sandra: *(Teasingly)* They're perfect, you know that. Just like us!

▸ *Drama Cue:*
All About the Dialogue

Dialogue is key here. Make sure your actors know their lines. The pace should be quick, conversational, and matter-of-fact. Help your actors focus on what's most important by not overblocking or characterizing their roles. Dialogue, dialogue, dialogue!

Jaden:	We're far from perfect . . . but maybe a little better than the rest of the family. The whole thing is a mystery to me.
Sandra:	What do you mean?
Jaden:	Why do married couples treat each other so poorly?
Sandra:	And how many years do you have to be married before you begin acting that way?
	(JADEN and SANDRA stop and look at each other for a moment.)
Jaden:	How long before you start calling me the "old man"?
Sandra:	And how long before you're ignoring me until you want your pot roast?
Jaden:	Are we only years away from a dysfunctional marriage?
Sandra:	Will we wish we were single?
Jaden:	This whole thing is a mystery!
Ben:	*(Spinning around)* Excuse me, I'm Ben. *(Moves around to the front row)* May I sit?
Jaden:	*(Taken by surprise)* Uh, sure.
Ben:	Thanks. I couldn't help but overhear your conversation. There is no secret to a happy marriage!
Linda:	*(Spinning around)* He's right. I'm Linda. *(Moves around to the front row)* May I sit?
Sandra:	Okay . . .
Linda:	Thanks. I was listening to your conversation, too. I agree marriage should not be a mystery.
Ben:	You are so right! *(Reaching across JADEN and SANDRA and shaking LINDA's hand)* I'm Ben.
Linda:	*(Shaking hands)* Linda. Flight 244?
Ben:	Flight 244. Did you hear these poor kids?
Linda:	There is nothing like a family reunion to make you question marriage.
	(JADEN and SANDRA have no idea what's going on. They are stunned but polite.)
Ben:	I don't know where Linda is coming from, but I believe a strong marriage is built on mutual respect, submission, and honor!
Linda:	*(Giving BEN a high five)* I'm right with you! *(To JADEN)* You're the head of the household. *(To SANDRA)* Does that make you mad?
Sandra:	No.

Linda:	That doesn't make you feel like less of a human being?
Sandra:	No, not really.
Ben:	*(To JADEN)* And do you like bossing your wife around?
Jaden:	Not bossing her around.
Ben:	Is that what's most important? Getting your needs met, all the while forgetting about her needs? *(To JADEN and SANDRA's horror, the questioning begins to come at them with a rapid-fire pace. The questions grow louder quickly build to a climax.)*
Jaden:	No, I've never been that way.
Linda:	Do you resent his leadership?
Sandra:	No.
Ben:	Do you resent her opinions?
Jaden:	No.
Ben:	Are you taking her to church each week?
Jaden:	Church? Yes.
Linda:	Do you resent your husband taking you to church each week?
Sandra:	No . . . we like going to church.
Jaden:	*(Finally)* Who are you, and why are you . . . ?
Ben:	Do you read the Bible?
Jaden:	Of course!
Linda:	Is he lying?
Sandra:	No! He reads the Bible! We both read the Bible!
Ben:	Do you honor you wife?
Jaden:	Yes!
Linda:	Do you honor your husband?
Sandra:	Yes!
Ben:	Do you love your wife as yourself?
Jaden:	I try.
Ben:	That's not good enough! Will you try harder?
Jaden:	Yes.
Linda:	Do you respect your husband in all things?
Sandra:	I said I did! Didn't I?

▸ *Caution: Overreactions*

When an exchange of dialogue happens between two characters, leaving other characters to react, be sure those reactions are subtle and do not upstage the dialogue. A couple of strategically placed BIG reactions will make for a stronger comedic or dramatic effect.

Ben:	Well, from what I see, you're going to make it!
Linda:	I agree! A perfect picture of Jesus and the church!
Ben:	Nothing to worry about!
Linda:	Your marriage will be just fine!
Ben:	*(Standing)* Linda, it was nice to meet you!
Linda:	*(Standing)* Nice to meet you too, Ben. See you on board?
Ben:	See you on board!
SOUND:	**MUSICAL TRANSITION OUT OF SKETCH**
	(They return to their seats, their backs facing the audience. JADEN and SANDRA just sit there in shock, not knowing what to say. After a few beats they look at each other . . .)
Jaden:	What just happened?
Sandra:	I think we just had some forced marriage counseling . . . from a couple of strangers . . . in an airport. Talk about weird.
Jaden:	And I thought marriage was mysterious!
Sandra:	Let's just hope we're not sitting next to them on the plane.
	MUSIC SWELLS
	(JADEN and SANDRA huddle together, somewhat in shock about what just happened.)
LIGHTS:	**FADE TO BLACK**
	END

DINING IN? OR TAKE-OUT?

TOPIC

Missions: Christians hoarding the Bread of Life and Living Water for themselves without caring about those around the world who are looking to be fed.

SYNOPSIS

Americans are gathered around the diner table indulging in a sumptuous meal of grace, forgiveness, peace, and fellowship. Behind them stand representatives from around the world who are hungry for spiritual food. The Americans are indifferent to the needs of the foreigners and justify their reasons why they do not take the "soul food" (gospel) to them. It is only after the Americans have had their fill and are ready to leave the table that the foreigners can come and eat the crumbs left behind.

SET/PROPS

A fully set dining table is needed. Bowls and platters of food need to be on the table. A raised platform should be upstage of the table for the international characters to stand on. Food will need to be available throughout the performance.

CHARACTERS

Sam

Amy

David

Cheryl

5 to 6 Internationals – Nonspeaking roles

LIGHTS:	**BLACKOUT** *(Actors move into place)*
SOUND:	**TRANSITION INTO SKETCH**
GRAPHIC:	**SLIDE #1—**
	This is that bread which came down from heaven: not as your fathers did eat manna, and are dead: he that eateth of this bread shall live forever. John 6:58
	SLIDE #2—
	Dining In? Or Take-Out?
LIGHTS:	**UP ON STAGE**

(We see SAM, AMY, DAVID, and CHERYL sitting around the table. Apparently the lavish meal they're enjoying is nearing an end. As they begin to speak, the lighting on the INTERNATIONALS behind them slowly comes up. During the course of the sketch, the INTERNATIONALS are watching the Americans eat. The INTERNATIONALS should appear hungry and weak. When someone from the table looks their way, they extend a hand out as if begging for food.)

Sam: We've outdone ourselves this time. This is the best meal yet!

Amy: Well, help yourself, there's plenty.

Cheryl: I'm stuffed!

David: Me too!

Amy: There's so much here.

David: *(Dipping more food on his plate)* I don't think I've ever tasted "grace" like this before!

Sam: *(Taking another spoonful of peas)* Or the "peace." It's beyond me how peace can be so fulfilling. I'll never understand how it's made . . . but it sure is good.

Amy: *(Referring to the meat on her plate)* The meat of God's Word is my favorite. It gives me the strength and energy I need to make it through the day. I can't get enough sometimes.

Cheryl: I know what you mean. *(Taking a dinner roll)* Mmmmm . . . the Bread of Life. I've not been the same since I tried it.

Sam: Isn't it wonderful that we have the opportunity to sit around the table together and be fed like this?

Amy: Amen.

(The group continues to ooh and ahh over their food.)

Sam: So, did anyone notice the *(inclining his head toward the INTERNATIONALS)* "you-know- who's" back there again?

Amy: Who invited them?

▸ *Drama Cue:*
Magic of Music

Find the right music to underscore your drama and then watch how it magically captures the hearts of your audience. Choose music that mirrors the emotions in action. Test the music by listening to it with your eyes closed. If the music helps you emotionally connect with what you know will take place onstage, you've found your selection.

David:	Don't look at me.
Cheryl:	No one has to invite them; they are always there.
Sam:	You're right . . . looking over our shoulders, watching us at the table.
Amy:	Just don't look at them . . . you'll forget they are there.
David:	What do they want, anyway?
Cheryl:	To be fed. They want what we have.
Sam:	But this is our food. I feel sorry for them, but we just happen to be born in the right country. It's not our fault.
Amy:	That's right . . . we're blessed of God.
David:	Could you pass the Living Water, please? It's not that I'm thirsty, I just can't get enough.

(A pitcher of water is passed to DAVID)

Sam:	Yep, we're fortunate people, all right.
Cheryl:	But I heard that we have a responsibility to share this with those around the world.
Amy:	I've sent a plate or two out to them.
David:	Our church sent this couple to take spiritual nourishment to some faraway land . . . but you know what happened . . .
Sam:	Hmm?
David:	They kept coming back asking for more. No matter how much we sent, there was always the need for more.
Amy:	And who knows what happens to that food once it leaves our table? How do we know it's even getting there?

(A few turn to look at the INTERNATIONALS)

Sam:	Don't look back there, I tell you. They'll get to you.
Cheryl:	It's too bad we couldn't do something. Maybe **each** of us could do more.
Amy:	Well, I don't know if you've noticed, but when I come to this table to eat, I usually end my prayers with something like "and I pray for the missionaries. Amen."
Sam:	What more can we do besides pray for them, send them a little take-out every now and then, and send them some more clothes?
David:	I'm all for that.
Cheryl:	But what if it is too late? What if they starve?

▶ *Caution:*
Music Mix-Ups

If a piece of instrumental music is to underscore dialogue of your actors, be sure that the music serves as a subtle background. Music that is too busy can fight with the spoken words of your actors.

Sam: *(Jokingly)* It's kind of hard to think about starving when you've just devoured so much you think you're going to burst.

(They all laugh)

David: I can't eat another bite.

Amy: Well, I hope you've left room for dessert.

Cheryl: Dessert?

Sam: What is it?

Amy: I've whipped up a little fellowship!

David: I'm in!

Amy: We'll serve it up on the terrace.

(Everyone gets up)

Sam: *(To Cheryl)* Lead the way, I'm right behind you.

David: Always room for dessert, right?

Amy: You go ahead, I'll be right there.

(SAM, CHERYL, and DAVID ad-lib conversationally as they exit. AMY tidies up the table. After a few beats, she wipes her hands on a napkin.)

Amy: *(Looking straight out into the audience)* We're finished now.

(AMY slowly exits)

SOUND: **INTERNATIONAL THEME**

(After AMY exits, the INTERNATIONALS look at the table. Slowly, one at a time, they venture off the platform and approach the table. They have come to take what is left behind. Each INTERNATIONAL should approach the table with a different emotion—fear, awe, illness, disappointment, etc. They rummage through the leftovers as . . .)

LIGHTS: **FADE TO BLACK**

SLIDES: **SLIDE #3—**
"Lovest thou Me? Feed My sheep." John 21:17

END

THE FINEST CHURCH IN AMERICA

TOPIC
Encouragement in the local church

SYNOPSIS
Alisa finds the characteristics of Christian love expressed more generously in the world than in the church she attends.

SET/PROPS
Church setting, choir risers to the side.

CHARACTERS
Young Alisa – 4 to 6 years old

Alisa – Disillusioned by the church

Edith – Church member

Ann – Church member

Paul – Church member

Charles – Church member

Rebecca – Church member

Lillian – Church member

LIGHTS:	**BLACKOUT** *(Actors move into place)*
GRAPHIC:	**TITLE SLIDE—** *The Finest Church in America*
MUSIC:	**TOY PIANO . . . "JESUS LOVES ME"** *(YOUNG ALISA should either be in a spotlight removed from the rest of the action or right at the feet of ALISA, who ends up SR of the congregation. The church members should be arranged on some sort of riser so they are grouped together, symbolizing a congregation.)*
Young Alisa:	*(Kneeling, doing the hand actions as she speaks)* Here's the church . . . here's the steeple . . . open the doors and look at all the *fine* people.
LIGHTS:	**FOLLOW-SPOT REMAINS ON YOUNG ALISA. BRING LIGHTS UP ON THE CHURCH CONGREGATION.** *(YOUNG ALISA continues to pantomime the "church" hand game . . .)*
Paul:	*(Focus to audience, but acting as if he is talking to EDITH)* Good morning, Edith. How are you today?
Edith:	Fine, and you?
Paul:	Fine . . . and how about you, Lillian?
Lillian:	I'm fine, thank you. Charles, good to see you in church this morning. How are you doing?
Charles:	Fine . . . really fine.
Lillian:	Oh . . . that's fine. And how is Ann?
Ann:	I'm fine too!
Lillian:	Oh, I didn't notice you standing there. How are you feeling?
Ann:	Fine . . . fine. Rebecca, don't you look lovely this morning! How's life treating you?
Rebecca:	Fine, thank you. And you?
Ann:	Really fine . . . thank you for asking.
Rebecca:	Alisa . . . I haven't seen you in ages. Heard you were having some trouble. How are you? *(ALISA begins to speak when the church members interrupt . . .)*
Edith:	She looks fine!
Ann:	She acts fine! *(Building . . .)*
Charles:	Fine!

▸ *Drama Cue:*
Center Stage

When performing a drama with a main character or narrator, place him in the middle of the action. Arrange the secondary characters around the leading role so the focus always returns to the center of the story.

Rebecca:	Fine!
Paul:	Fine!
Lillian:	Isn't this a fine Sunday!
LIGHTS:	**LIGHTS DIM ON CONGREGATION ... FOLLOW-SPOT ON ALISA**
	(The CHURCH MEMBERS freeze ... as ALISA pulls away from the group and addresses the audience.)
Alisa:	As you can see, I go to the "fine-est" church in America. Everything is fine! Well, actually, everything is **not** fine, but the congregation is a lot happier when they believe everything is "fine." You see, if you believe everyone around you is fine, then you won't have to go out of your way to help or encourage anyone. I was always taught that the church was your family. When you hurt, everyone hurt with you. When you needed support, your Christian brothers and sisters would be there to lift you up. It didn't take very long to realize that wasn't always true.
LIGHTS:	**LIGHTS TO FULL ON CONGREGATION**
Edith:	Did you hear about Alisa? She's going through a real hard time.
Ann:	Bless her heart. Do you think we should call her?
Paul:	*(Not wanting to be inconvenienced)* Uh ... she probably would rather be left alone.
Lillian:	*(More than happy to agree with Paul)* You're right ... she does live a long way from the church.
Charles:	You're not kidding! It would be kind of inconvenient to drive out there.
Rebecca:	Do you suppose one of us should call her? See if she is okay?
	(Pause)
All:	She'll be fine.
LIGHTS:	**DIM ON CONGREGATION**
Alisa:	But I wasn't fine. I did get through that trial, but sadly, with no help from my church family. Those problems seemed insignificant to the ones I knew other church members were having. There were many in our congregation struggling with sin who needed the unconditional love that could encourage them back to Jesus. They seldom received that love ...
LIGHTS:	**LIGHTS TO FULL ON CONGREGATION**
Edith:	Who would have ever thought? A sinner in this church!
Ann:	The church is hardly a place for sinners!

Paul:	I think we should leave them alone until they get their lives straightened out.
Lillian:	But what if I run into them at the supermarket? *(Rethinking her position)* Wait a minute. Why should I be worried? They're the sinner, not me!
Charles:	Let's hope that someone can help them. Maybe there's a good Christian book on that particular problem?
Rebecca:	Do you suppose one of us should go to them? Maybe we could call them, or drop them a note . . . show them some unconditional love.
	(Pause)
All:	They'll be fine.
Alisa:	But they weren't fine. And that avoidance encouraged them to run right into the open arms of the world. The world cared for them more than the church. Encouraging others takes unconditional love, acceptance, and yes, sometimes to be inconvenienced.
LIGHTS:	**LIGHTS TO FULL ON CONGREGATION**
Edith:	If I knew of someone to encourage, I would! But I'm not going to stick my nose in other people's business!
Ann:	I work forty hours a week. Why should I be expected to "spread sunshine" about the congregation? No one ever encourages me!
Paul:	Personally, I would want to be left alone . . . because I'm like that, I expect other people to be like that as well.
Lillian:	Listen, half of people's problems are brought on by themselves. If they wouldn't do some of the things they do, they wouldn't be in these predicaments. It's their own fault.
Charles:	The church isn't a place for support, love, hugs, and all that mushy stuff. We're here to learn about Jesus!
Rebecca:	But wasn't Jesus an encourager? Didn't He touch others and verbally express His feelings? Maybe that's what we need?
	(Pause)
All:	No, we're fine!
LIGHTS:	**LIGHTS DIM ON CONGREGATION**
Alisa:	The church is full of hurting people. The congregation is made up of sinners. The members aren't immune to depression and emotional problems. When will we ever learn that? When will we see our responsibility? When will be honest with each other?
	(Turns to CONGREGATION)
	Really, how are you?
LIGHTS:	**LIGHTS UP ON CONGREGATION**

▶ *Caution: Reader's Theater*

Reader's Theater should not sound like you are reading. Make sure your actors are familiar with their script! They may assume that the rehearsal commitment will not be as exacting as for a regular drama performance, but in some ways Reader's Theater takes *more* work to sound conversational than with a memorized script.

Edith: *(Hurting)* My marriage is breaking up.

Ann: My father's dying.

Paul: *(Humbly)* I just filed for bankruptcy.

Lillian: My daughter ran away from home.

Charles: I have a drinking problem.

Rebecca: I'm losing my job.

Alisa: *(Walking back into the group)* So . . . how are you?

MUSIC: **"Jesus Loves Me" music box**

All: *(Without emotion)* Fine.

LIGHTS: **LIGHTS DIM ON CONGREGATION. FOLLOW UP SOFT ON YOUNG ALISA.**

Young Alisa: Here's the church . . . here's the steeple . . . open the doors and there's all the fine people.

LIGHTS: **FADE TO BLACK**

END

LOVE HANDLES

TOPIC
The love of God: Loving others in spite of themselves

SCRIPTURE
I John 4:8; I Corinthians 13:1, 13

SYNOPSIS
Carla is seeking unconditional love. Many candidates come her way.
She could find it in herself to love and accept them, but when they see
that Carla carries "baggage" in her life, they quickly reject her.
Ultimately, she continues in her search for unconditional love.

SET/PROPS
The stage should be set with a bench for Carla to sit on. Next to the bench
should be some sort of table or risers on which Carla's suitcases can be
placed. Six pieces of luggage, different sizes, are needed. Each piece of
luggage should have a word printed on the side: "Past," "Needs,"
"Imperfections," "Appearance" (this one should be a vanity case),
"Mistakes," "Values," and "Dreams."

CHARACTERS

Carla – 20s to 30s; nice, pleasant, honest

Charlie – street person

Sarah – 30+; pleasant, selfish, thoughtless

Stephen – 20s to 30s; cool, collected, smooth

Terry – 20+; judgmental, unforgiving

LIGHTING:	**BLACKOUT (Actors move into place)**
SOUND:	**MUSICAL TRANSITION INTO SCENE**
GRAPHIC:	**SLIDE 1—** *Love Handles*
LIGHTING:	**LIGHTS UP - SR**

(As lights come up, we see CARLA pacing the floor next to her luggage. Each suitcase has been placed so that the audience is unable to see the signs which state the contents of each case. CARLA checks the time by her watch. CHARLIE enters . . .)

CHARLIE: Hey, Miss Carla. I see you're back again today.

CARLA: Yeah, I think today's going to be my lucky day.

CHARLIE: Why?

CARLA: Just a feeling, I guess. Besides I don't know what I'm going to do if I can't find someone who'll love me. Charlie, I've been looking for love for a very long time now. Surely, it's out there, somewhere.

CHARLIE: It is . . . somewhere. I'll talk to you soon.

(CHARLIE exits . . . CARLA continues to pace. SARAH enters.)

CARLA: Sarah! Are you ever a sight for sore eyes. Is it you I'm looking for?

SARAH: I'm not for sure what you're looking for, but your big sister will do her best!

CARLA: I'm looking for someone who will love me.

SARAH: Carla, I'm family . . . of course I love you . . . get your things and come on with me.

CARLA: Well, I have a lot of baggage here I have to take with me. Like this one. *(Picks up suitcase labeled "Dreams")* These are all my dreams for my life. I want them all to come true.

SARAH: That's fine. Let me help you.

(SARAH crosses and begins to help CARLA with her luggage.)

CARLA: I knew I could count on you guys. I mean, if you can't count on your family, then who can you . . .

SARAH: *(Turning a suitcase around that reads "Mistakes")* What is this?

CARLA: Oh, it's just part of my life.

SARAH: Mistakes.

CARLA: I've made lots of them when I left home. Even leaving home was a mistake.

▸ *Drama Cue:*
Reading 101

In this sketch the script calls for signs to be placed on each piece of luggage. Be sure to make them large enough for your audience to read clearly. Use bold lettering and stay away from too elaborate a script. Simple and bold is the best rule here.

SARAH:	But Carla . . . all these mistakes?
CARLA:	I know I made many, and even though I'm moving on, I will never be able to recover from some of the mistakes I've made.
SARAH:	*(Reaching down and taking another suitcase)* And these are your values?
CARLA:	Yes, they go with me as well.
SARAH:	But these are so different than ours.
CARLA:	I'm sorry. I know we won't agree in every one of these areas. *(Trying to break the tension)* But anyway, I'll be glad to carry these two cases if you would rather . . .
SARAH:	Carla, I'm sorry. This just isn't going to work. You're too . . . too . . .
CARLA:	Different from the family. Sarah, all of this is who I am. You can't love me in spite of that?
SARAH:	*(Looks at watch)* Oops! Gotta go. See you at Thanksgiving. Bye-bye!
	(SARAH blows her a kiss, then exits. STEVEN enters.)
STEVEN:	*(Notices the pretty gal)* Hello—who are you?
CARLA:	I'm Carla.
STEVEN:	Who are waiting for?
CARLA:	Someone who will love me.
STEVEN:	I'm looking for someone to love. You interested in a happy marriage and spending a lifetime together?
CARLA:	Yes, I just want to be loved.
STEVEN:	Then let's go. *(He moves to take some of the luggage)*
CARLA:	I know we are going to be very happy.
STEVEN:	What's in here? *(He turns suitcase around . . . it reads "Needs")* You have needs?
CARLA:	Yes.
STEVEN:	*(Losing interest)* Oh . . . a lot?
CARLA:	A few.
STEVEN:	Is it necessary to take them along?
CARLA:	I would like to. They are a part of who I really am.
STEVEN:	*(Picking up the vanity case that reads "Appearance")* And what's in this case? It's so heavy.
CARLA:	I'll want to look nice for you.

▸ *Caution: Object Lesson*

Prop-intensive dramas are nothing more than an object lesson presented theater style. Specific props featured in each script represent something with meaning. Actors need to understand that the props are telling the story just as much as their dialogue.

STEVEN:	You mean it's going to take all this for you to look good?
CARLA:	And probably more as the years go by.
STEVEN:	*(Noticeable change in him as he sets down the case)* Look, maybe I was a little hasty. You're a nice girl, but I didn't realize that you came with so much . . . uh . . .
CARLA:	Baggage?
STEVEN:	Uh . . . yeah.
CARLA:	*(Holding up the "Dreams" suitcase)* I guess you wouldn't be interested in my dreams either.
STEVEN:	I just don't think I am a part of your dream.
CARLA:	You're right. You're not.
	(STEVEN exits. CARLA looks very discouraged. TERRY enters, carrying a Bible in hand.)
TERRY:	Excuse me, is something wrong?
CARLA:	Other than the fact that I can't seem to find true love, no.
TERRY:	It's rough out here, huh?
CARLA:	I guess so. All I find is "I love you because" . . . or "I love you if . . . "
TERRY:	Listen, there is a group of us who fellowship at a church down the street. Why don't you come join us?
CARLA:	Will I find love there?
TERRY:	You'll know we're Christians by our love! Let's go.
CARLA:	It sounds too good to be true. That's what I've always dreamed about.
TERRY:	Let me help you with this big suitcase. *(Turns it around)* Wait a minute. You didn't tell me about this.
CARLA:	My past?
TERRY:	*(Opening the suitcase)* What's in here?
CARLA:	Please don't open it!
TERRY:	*(Look inside . . . stunned)* You've done all of this?
CARLA:	I'm not proud of it! Nonetheless, it *is* my past. I've been forgiven for everything I've done, but I will never be able to erase the memories or the consequences of my sin. My past will always be baggage in my life.
TERRY:	*(Taking the last suitcase)* And this . . . this isn't very good either. You're, well . . . imperfect.
SOUND:	**CLOSING MUSIC TO BLACKOUT**

CARLA: Can you and your church friends love the unlovely? There are a lot of us out here. In the streets, or in a support group, or in a hospice dying. We are all looking for just a little unconditional love. Tell me, is our baggage too much for you to handle?

TERRY: Don't preach to me, sister. I may not be perfect, but I've never done the things you've done.

CARLA: I'm not asking for your approval, just your love.

(TERRY, having no reply, exits. CARLA takes another look at her watch. Begins to organize her luggage to leave. CHARLIE enters.)

CHARLIE: Calling it a day?

CARLA: *(Dejectedly)* Yeah. You know, Charlie, I think I'm looking for love in all the wrong places.

CHARLIE: Maybe tomorrow. You're a great gal.

CARLA: A great gal, but when you get me, you get all of this. *(Motions to her baggage)*

(As CARLA exist the stage with all her suitcases, CHARLIE notices she has left behind the case that reads "Dreams.")

CHARLIE: Hey, wait a minute. You left this one behind.

CARLA: No, just leave it. I need to travel light, and it looks like I won't need that suitcase anyway. Good night, Charlie.

(CARLA and CHARLIE exit the stage in different directions. MUSIC SWELLS . . . and light remains up on the "Dream" suitcase. And as the lights fade . . .)

LIGHTING: FADE TO BLACK

GRAPHIC: SLIDE 2—
"God IS Love." I John 4:8

END

Putting Your Best Faith Forward

TOPIC
Faith

SCRIPTURE
Hebrews 11:4

SYNOPSIS
Jerry is putting his best faith forward when it comes to giving to God. His sacrifice upsets his family, because their faith is next to nothing. The family can't understand why Jerry would give so much to God, when God hasn't even asked him for such a sacrifice.

CHARACTERS
Jerry – strong faith

Dan – Jerry's brother

Gail – Jerry's sister

Deb – Jerry's sister

Mom – Jerry's mom

SETS/PROPS

A table covered with a black or gold tablecloth, four large solid-colored shopping bags, four small wrapped gifts, and very large wrapped gift (this last should be filled with six to seven small gifts).

LIGHTS:	**BLACKOUT** *(Actors move into place)*
SOUND:	**MUSICAL TRANSITION INTO SKETCH**
GRAPHIC:	**TITLE SLIDE—** *Putting Your Best Faith Forward*
LIGHTS:	**UP ON STAGE**

(We see a table draped in a black/gold tablecloth in front and CS. Enter DAN, GAIL, DEB, and MOM. They each carry a large solid-colored shopping bag. They are dressed very nicely, as if they are going to a special event. They stop far back behind the table . . .)

Mom: Look, kids, let's just do this and get it over with. You know the drill.

Dan: We know the drill.

Gail: It should be a little different this year, being that this is the first time Jerry will get to participate.

Deb: Jerry. Where's Jerry?

Mom: He called and said he would meet us here.

Dan: So where is he?

Mom: I knew I should have insisted that we come as a family.

Dan: I've got a feeling Jerry is going to mess this whole thing up!

Gail: Hey, give him a break. He's a new Christian.

Dan: Yeah, well, like I said, I've got a real bad feeling!

(Jerry enters empty-handed)

Jerry: Hi, Mom, everybody!

Mom: Jerry, you're late!

Jerry: Actually, I've been here for a while. I just was taking a look around, waiting for all of you to show up.

Deb: Jerry, didn't you bring your . . .

Jerry: I've taken care of it.

Mom: Good. Now remember, kids, short and sweet and we'll be on our way. How about I start?

Gail: Go ahead, Mom.

Mom: *(Steps to the table)* Hello, God. It's me. Of course You know who I am. Anyway, I wanted to give You something, a token of my appreciation and love for You.

(MOM reaches into her bag, takes out a wrapped gift, and places it on the table.)

Nice, huh? You're welcome! *(Turns)* Next!

▶ *Drama Cue:*
Giving Directions

When actors speak up and out to God, predetermine exactly where they should look. Find a place out above the audience where the characters can focus. Make this the spot where the unseen character in the sketch resides. A little direction about this focus is key to uniformity.

Gail:	And this is from me. *(Takes her gift out of the bag and places it on the table)* Pretty cool, huh?
Deb:	*(Reaches into her bag and takes out a gift)* For You. I thought You'd like this better than what I gave You last year.
Dan:	*(Takes his gift out of his bag)* Dan's back! And look what I'm giving You. A sacrifice, I know, but hey, I'm Dan!
Mom:	*(To JERRY)* Just do what the rest of us did. Walk up and give your gift—that's it.
Jerry:	That's it?
Mom:	You did bring your gift, didn't you?

(JERRY nods. MOM walks back up to the table.)

As You know, my son is new at all of this. Well, of course You know. Anyway, be patient with him. Jerry?

(JERRY walks to the table and looks up.)

Jerry:	God, You've given me so much. I want to give You something special in return.

(JERRY reaches down under the table, brings up a very large gift that is beautifully wrapped, and places it on the table.)

It's nothing compared to what You've given to me, but it is Yours to have.

(The rest of JERRY's family is stunned by JERRY's gift. They run to the table and grab JERRY.)

Gail:	*(Looking heavenward)* We'll be right back.

(GAIL, DEB, DAN, and MOM drag JERRY back)

Mom:	What in the world are you doing?
Jerry:	The same thing you all were doing!
Dan:	No. We certainly didn't do *(Points)* that!
Jerry:	What's wrong? What did I do?
Mom:	Look, Jerry, you went a little overboard!
Deb:	You didn't have to give Him that much of your life!
Jerry:	But I wanted to.
Gail:	That was way too much. Very inappropriate!
Mom:	Jerry, son, let me give you a little bit of motherly advice. If God didn't ask for all that, don't give it! It's too costly!
Dan:	Save a little for yourself. If He wants more, He'll tell you!

▸ *Caution: Attention to Details*

A great sketch can be sabotaged by failing to pay adequate attention to the details. Make a list of the little things that make up the big picture. Details in blocking, props, sets, and other important elements of stage production will not go unnoticed by your audience.

Deb:	You have to pace yourself, Jerry! Pace yourself.
Mom:	*(Walks over and takes the package off the table)* God, I think Jerry is reconsidering this sacrifice. Can You just give us a few minutes to talk him through this?
	(MOM walks back to the group with the gift.)
Jerry:	*(Grabbing the gift out of MOM's hands)* I am not reconsidering my sacrifice. I want to give this to God!
Gail:	But God didn't require that of you!
Dan:	An eighth of that would be a great gesture of faith, in my book!
Jerry:	Sorry. No offense, but this is what I want to do.
	(Walks to the table with the gift, then sets the gift on the table and returns to the group.)
Mom:	I get it! I know what you're trying to do! You're trying to show up the rest of us with this great sacrifice you've given!
Dan:	Mom's exactly right. We bring a sufficient sacrifice, then you walk in with your large sacrifice and make us look bad!
Jerry:	I'm not trying to make you look bad.
Gail:	Yes you are!
Jerry:	I'm not trying to embarrass you. I am only trying to put my best faith forward! I couldn't do enough for God. It's up to Him how He blesses me in return.
Deb:	You can fool us, but you can't fool God.
Jerry:	I am not trying to fool anyone! And if it is the heart God judges, doesn't He see your motives as well?
Mom:	Don't be lecturing us about motives. Now, I think Jerry has humiliated us enough before God for one day! Let's get out of here.
	(Everyone begins to leave, but JERRY walks back to the table. The others stop to listen.)
Jerry:	*(Looks heavenward)* God, I didn't do this for show. I gave having faith You would be honored. I hope You are.
Mom:	Jerry! C'mon.
SOUND:	**MUSICAL TRANSITION OUT OF SKETCH**
	(Everyone once again begins to exit, then MOM stops and walks back to the table and looks up to heaven. She points to her gift . . .)
	May I remind you that good things come in small packages!
	(She returns and GAIL walks to the table.)

Gail: *(Looking upward as she points to her gift)* Remember, it's the thought that counts!

(GAIL walks to group as DEB goes to the table.)

Deb: *(Looking upward)* Look, if You gave me a little more, I could give You a little more back!

Dan: *(Jumps in)* Ditto!

(The group finally makes their exit. DAN trails the rest and after the others have moved offstage, DAN returns. He goes to the table and takes JERRY's gift, looks both ways, and puts it back under the table. He then rearranges the gifts on the table, leaving his gift in the middle. He smiles as he reviews his handiwork, then looks up to God and gives God a big wink. DAN exits stage . . .)

LIGHTS: FADE TO BLACK

END

HALL OF PRAYERS

"Lord, Teach Us to Pray!"

TOPIC

Prayer

SYNOPSIS

Take a trip down the Hall of Prayers, where every type of prayer
is heard except for the right prayer. Finally, the plea goes out . . .
"Lord, teach us to pray!"

**Note: This drama is the perfect introduction to a message
on the Lord's Prayer.**

SETS/PROPS

No definite stage or set is required. Chairs and platforms can be used
to designate different characters' homes, etc.

CHARACTERS

Narrator

Frantic – Emergency Room prayer

Shopper – Shopping List prayer

Sleeper – Rip van Winkle prayer

Whiner – The Whiner's prayer

Orator – The Waxing Eloquent but Going Nowhere prayer

LIGHTS:	BLACKOUT *(Actors move into place)*
ORGAN:	TRANSITION INTO DRAMA: "Sweet Hour of Prayer" on organ. Organ continues to play throughout each prayer . . . with a little variation in the theme to go along with the type of prayer.
Narrator:	Welcome to the Hall of Prayers. It is in this hall that we hear the way we pray . . . but are any of these prayers the perfect prayer? Let's find out . . . let's first listen to the all-so-familiar Emergency Room prayer.
SOUND:	**EMERGENCY SIREN**
ORGAN:	CONTINUES "Sweet Hour of Prayer," but now plays it in a minor key throughout the Emergency Room prayer.
LIGHTS:	UP on THE FRANTIC *(Maybe SPFX red flashing light across the stage)*
Frantic:	*(Stands and delivers pray out and upwards. Pacing and pleading)* Oh, Father . . . it's me again! It seems that every time I get around to talking to You, it is the result of some tragedy in my life. Well, here I am again. You've got to help me! I'm desperate! In case You haven't noticed, I've got big problems here! My whole world is crumbling around me! *(Bargaining)* Look, I know I've told You this before, but Lord, if You'll just help me out of this mess, I'll serve You for the rest of my life. No . . . I mean it! I'll do anything for You . . . I'll even go to Africa as a missionary! So c'mon, what do You say? Huh? Be a sport! *(Listens)* Okay . . . see You at the next crisis!
ORGAN:	**RESUME REGULAR MELODY**
LIGHTS:	**BLACKOUT**
Narrator:	Yes, the Emergency Room prayer. And haven't we all prayed this next prayer . . . the Shopping List prayer!
LIGHTS:	**UP ON THE SHOPPER**
Shopper:	*(With Bible in hand)* Okay, I don't have much time, but I'm coming before You, Lord, with a heavy heart . . . and a very long list. *(Opens Bible—and a huge list unfolds out of the Bible and streams down to the floor)* First of all . . . it's my job. I need a new one. I can't take it at that office anymore. And if I'm going to have a new job, I should really get a new car. Mine's so old! I certainly can't be a good testimony for You riding around in that old heap. And I'll need new clothes for my new job. And actually, if I get a new job, I'd like it to be downtown. That means, Father, You're going to have to provide a brand-new home for me in the downtown district! And because I'm sure my new job will be stressful . . . *(Slight pause)* Well, Father, could you provide a Jacuzzi too?
LIGHTS:	**BLACKOUT**

▸ *Drama Cue: Congregational Chuckle*

I encourage you to go larger than life here. Dress up each character by using hand props and costumes that emphasize who they represent. This will help the audience understand that you're *poking* fun, not *making* fun.

Narrator:	Now hold on to your seats . . . and stay alert. Here comes the prayer most of have prayed, many times: the Rip van Winkle prayer!
LIGHTS:	**UP ON SLEEPER**
ORGAN:	**"Sweet Hour of Prayer" transforms into the "Go to Sleep" lullaby**
Sleeper:	*(Kneels at the edge of a chair')* Okay! *(Yawns)* Here we go. *(Checks watch)* Whew! Okay, here we go. Dear heavenly Father . . . I come before You this morning to pray about . . . *(drops into a dazed/sleepy trance)* . . . You know . . . okay . . . I'm sorry for my shortcomings . . . and I want to thank You for my . . . comfortable bed . . . *(Yawns, begins nodding off. As SLEEPER's head bobs down and hits chin to chest, he/she wakes up, startled)* Oh . . . pray for the missionaries . . . and *(Yawns . . . then slaps both cheeks to wake up)* Kneel! I need to kneel. *(Kneels and places head on the soft chair)* Lord, I want to thank You for this nice, comfortable chair. It's so . . . *(Begins to doze off)* Okay . . . okay . . . now, where was . . . oh, yeah, I pray for . . . I pray for . . . I pray for . . . *(Begins to fade again. Head bobs downward and is again startled awake . . . almost shouts)* "And to the Republic for which it stands . . . one nation under God . . . and the Word was with God . . . God is good, God is great . . . (slipping away again) . . . thank You for this food . . . (Again nods off to sleep . . . head and body start swaying . . . finally lands face first in the chair. Begins to snore loudly)*
LIGHTS:	**BLACKOUT**
ORGAN:	**RESUMES MELODY (ADD VIOLIN)**
Narrator:	As we continue down the Hall of Prayers, let us stop and listen to the Whiner's Prayer!
Whiner:	Father, why me? I mean, really. Isn't it someone else's turn to have something go wrong? Everything that can go bad goes bad for me. It's just not fair! Can't You see? I mean, really! I keep having these terrible headaches. And chronic indigestion on top of that! So why me? I mean, really! Isn't it someone else's turn to have something go wrong? Am I being punished for something? What did I ever do to deserve this? I'm a good guy, right? Hello? Hello? God, are You even listening to me? It's me, Pete.
LIGHTS:	**BLACKOUT**
ORGAN:	**MELODY IN CATHEDRAL STYLE**
Narrator:	And haven't we all been taken captive by this next prayer, the Waxing Eloquent but Going Nowhere prayer!
Orator:	*(Walks up to a microphone on a stand; acts dramatic and theatrical)* The pastor has personally requested me to lead us to the throne of grace in prayer this morning. Let us bow before Him. *(Prayer can actually be read from a card in ORATOR's hand.)*

(Silent . . . then breaking into a theatrical soliloquy) Father, Thou art Thou, and we acknowledge that Thou art Thou, Father! And it is to Thee, Thou Father that we say, we love Thee, Father. And Father, because Thou art Thou, and we knowest Thou art Thou, we love to seek Thee among Thou people. Father, because Thou art Thou . . . Thou sanctified saints come into Thine house and kneel before Thine throne, Father . . . because of Thy Thouness! Father, as You see, so many are not in Thy house on this day, O Father, so bless our dedication. For we humbly pray to You today, Thou Father, our Father, because I and the others here acknowledge that Thou art Thou, Father. Bless this prayer!

Sleeper: *(Lets out a deep snore)*

(The ORATOR is offended and looks at the sleeping prayer warrior in stern amazement.)

ORGAN: **"THE LORD's PRAYER"** *(Until end of sketch)*

LIGHTS: **BLACKOUT**

Narrator: How did you enjoy our tour through the Hall of Prayers? Though every prayer was different, was any one of them the perfect prayer?

LIGHTS: **UP ON STAGE: FULL GROUP**

Frantic: The perfect prayer? I know my prayer wasn't perfect, but it was definitely important to me!

Whiner: The perfect prayer? I'm not so sure my prayers go any further than the ceiling and bounce right back down on me. *(Dawns on him)* Maybe that's why I have those headaches.

Shopper: The perfect prayer? My prayers are perfectly organized and perfectly thought out . . . so what's wrong with my prayer?

Orator: The perfect prayer? *(Arrogantly)* Why, weren't you listening? I just prayed it!

Sleeper: *(Snore)*

(The whole group turns and looks at the SLEEPER. Then they turn to the audience)

All: Lord, teach us to pray!

MUSIC: **SWELLS AS LIGHTS FADE**

LIGHTS: **FADE TO BLACK**

END

▸ *Caution: Transitions*

Scene transitions within a sketch can really cause a drama to drag. Instead of changing scenes through the use of a curtain or lights, try placing all your characters onstage at the same time; have them come to life only when they speak their lines.

Eternally Yours

TOPIC

Worship: Living a life of continuous worship as a result of living life with an eternal perspective.

SYNOPSIS

John Williams's staff is in a dither. When John's staff finds his misplaced Day Planner, they become worried! Two words appear on almost every page in his calendar: *Eternal Perspective.* What does this mean? John's staff fears the worst, but after John explains he is trying to focus on worshiping God in everything he does and everywhere he goes, his staff is relieved.

CAST

Carol – John's administrative assistant

Tara – Office staff worker

Jimmy Ray – Maintenance worker

Mr. Williams – Executive

SETS/PROPS

Sketch takes place in an office. Props: desk chairs, desk accessories, briefcase, and Day Planner.

LIGHTS:	BLACKOUT *(Actors move into place)*
SOUND:	TRANSITION MUSIC INTO SKETCH
GRAPHIC:	TITLE SLIDE— *Eternally Yours*
LIGHTS:	UP ON STAGE

(CAROL, TARA, and JIMMY RAY are all gathered in MR. WILLIAMS's office. They appear to be concerned and nervous. CAROL is standing behind the desk. TARA is distraught, with her hand over her mouth; she is holding back tears. JIMMY RAY is nervously explaining to them what he found in the parking lot.)

▶ *Drama Cue: Clues*

Most dramas offer clues to characterization of each role. They can be found in parenthetical direction, dialogue interaction, frame of thought, emotional reaction, and interaction between characters. Identify the clues in your script and build your characters from there.

Jimmy Ray: So there it was. Lying in a big puddle of grease in the middle of the parking lot.

Tara: I just can't believe this!

Jimmy Ray: I picked it up thinking it was some yahoo's Day Planner . . . little did I know . . .

Carol: It must have fallen out of his car when he left work last night.

Jimmy Ray: I wasn't trying to be nosy. I just waned to know who it belonged to.

Carol: Jimmy Ray, you did the right thing by looking inside.

Jimmy Ray: But that's when I saw all that horrible stuff written in there.

Tara: What are we going to do? This is tragic! And why Mr. Williams, of all people? He's such a wonderful Christian man!

Carol: Tara, pull yourself together! There must be some explanation for this!

Tara: *(Referring to the Day Planner)* You see what's written in there! What else could it all mean?

Carol: Now we've just speculated on what it means. We won't actually know until we ask him.

Jimmy Ray: I'm not asking him.

Tara: I'm not asking him either!

Jimmy Ray: You're his secretary!

Carol: But you're the one that found his Day Planner!

Jimmy Ray: He'd take it better coming from you!

Tara: Yeah, you ask him!

Williams: *(Entering)* Ask me what?

(CAROL, TARA, and JIMMY DEAN react nervously to MR. WILLIAMS's arrival.)

Jimmy Ray:	Nothing. I've got to go.
Tara:	Me too.
	(TARA and JIMMY DEAN head for the door . . .)
Williams:	Why are you three all standing in my office?
Carol:	Mr. Williams, have you been looking for your Day Planner?
Williams:	Yes, I have.
Carol:	After work yesterday, Jimmy Ray found it lying in the middle of the parking lot.
Jimmy Ray:	I degreased it for you, Mr. Williams.
Williams:	Why, thank you, Jimmy Ray.
Carol:	We must confess that we looked inside to make sure it was yours. We were going to call security, but . . .
	(TARA starts crying . . .)
Williams:	What's wrong with her?
Tara:	Mr. Williams, it has been a pleasure working for you, and I will always remember you as a kind, generous, thoughtful Christian.
Jimmy Ray:	And when I remember you, I will always think of how tidy you kept your office. And the nice Christmas ham you gave my family last year.
Williams:	*(Looking to CAROL for an explanation)* Are they going somewhere?
Carol:	*(Getting emotional)* No, but apparently you are!
Williams:	What are you talking about?
Carol:	*(Picking up the Day Planner)* It's all right here. We didn't mean to spy, but we couldn't help but see what was written on almost every day of your calendar.
Tara:	Are you in pain?
Jimmy Ray:	How long have you got?
Carol:	You're a brave man, Mr. Williams.
Williams:	*(Walking around to his desk)* Would someone like to explain what's going on here?
Carol:	*(Moving around to stand by the other two)* Eternal perspective! It's written all over your Day Planner.
Williams:	Yeah, so?
Carol:	When were you going to tell us?

▸ *Caution:*
Situation Tragedy

Situation comedy is funny because it represents a slice of real life! One caution: Keep your characters real so that your audience will connect with them. You can turn a comedy into a tragedy if you go for gags and slapstick instead of relying on the strong comedic quality of the situation.

Williams:	Wait a minute. You three think I'm terminally ill? Look, I am on my way to heaven, but I don't plan to go anytime soon.
Tara:	But we thought you were sick—that you could be taken into eternity any day!
Williams:	That's true of any of us, but that's not why I have *eternal perspective* written in my Day Planner. *(Picks up Day Planner)* It's written there to remind me to live each day with eternity in mind! Every day of my life should be spent worshiping my heavenly Father! And that means I worship God wherever I go, and in whatever I do.
Carol:	But you have it written above your office meetings, your vacation schedule . . . even your dental appointment!
Williams:	You're exactly right! In everything I do, I can find a way to worship and fellowship with God. And that doesn't start the day I die; it starts while I'm alive.
	(CAROL, TARA, and JIMMY RAY look at each other for moment.)
Jimmy Ray:	Mr. Williams, I knew what was going on, but these two . . . well, you know women.
Williams:	I am eternally His, and I live each moment with an eternal perspective on life. What good is everything I do today if it doesn't matter for tomorrow!
SOUND:	**MUSICAL TRANSITION OUT OF SKETCH**
Jimmy Ray:	Well, I've gotta get going. There's an air conditioning problem on the third floor! There's a bird or something stuck in the vent . . . glad everything's okay, boss.
	(JIMMY RAY exits. TARA, still with her hand over her mouth, is now crying tears of joy. She walks over to MR. WILLIAMS, pats his hand, turns, and exits.)
Williams:	*(Under his breath)* Oh, boy.
Carol:	*(Begins to leave, then turns back to MR. WILLIAMS)* Mr. Williams, I'm glad everything is okay. And if my opinion matters, your life does reflect a life of worship.
Williams:	Thank you, Carol.
Carol:	And should I order you a rubber stamp?
Williams:	A rubber stamp? What would it say?
Carol:	*Eternal Perspective*. It could save you a lot of writing.
	(CAROL and WILLIAMS smile at one another, then CAROL exits as . . .)
LIGHTS:	**FADE TO BLACK**
	END

GLOSSARY OF TERMS

Acting Area. The area of the stage setting on which the actor performs (may include areas off the normal stage). Usually split into portions for ease of reference: Up Stage, Center Stage, Stage Right, Stage Left, Apron, Offstage, etc.

Ad-Lib. Unrehearsed lines spoken during a performance 1) in reaction to other lines or 2) to transition from a mistake or dropped lines.

Aisle. A passage through seating.

Apron. Section of the stage floor which projects toward or into the auditorium. In proscenium theaters, the part of the stage in front of the main stage.

Aside. Lines spoken by an actor directly to the audience, not meant to be "heard" by other characters onstage.

Audition. Process where the director or casting director of a production asks performers to show what they can do. Tests the actors' response to a piece of text not prepared beforehand.

Backstage. The part of the stage and theater which is out of the sight of the audience; the service areas of the theater.

Beat. Short amount of time for a character to react, think, or pause in dialogue; smallest division of action in a play.

Blackout. A total, sometimes sudden, extinguishing of the stage lights, often at the end of a scene or act.

Blocking. The art of moving actors on and off the stage. This helps familiarize actors with their entrance and exit points. Also, the process of roughing out the moves as one actor relates to another in crossing the stage, sitting, standing, and all other actions.

"Break a Leg." A superstitious and widely accepted alternative to "Good luck" (which is considered bad luck in the theater).

Breaking Character. When actors do or say something inconsistent with the character they are portraying.

Call (Call Time). Notification of when production team, actors, and crew are scheduled to begin a rehearsal or performance.

Cast. The performers onstage.

Casting. The process the director goes through in choosing actors to perform the characters in a play.

Center Stage (CS). The middle portion of the stage—has good sightlines to all seats in the auditorium.

"Cheat Out" or "Open Up." This is simply a request for the actor to face more toward the audience. Although it is natural for people to face each other in real life, onstage the actor needs to make sure the audience can see and hear him or her.

Choreographer. Member of the production team responsible for setting dances and movement sequences during the production.

Comic Relief. A comic scene (or line) included in an otherwise straight-faced play to provide a relief from tension for the audience.

Costumes. Clothes worn by the actors onstage.

Cover. To make up dialogue and or blocking due to a mistake or accident onstage without breaking character.

Cross. The movement of an actor across the stage in any direction.

Cue. A signal to begin movement or speaking. There are many different types of cues. One is where an actor's cue to move or speak is dictated by the line (sentence) or word spoken by another actor. Another cue is when movement or speech is determined by sound/music or change in lighting. Sometimes an actor's cue will be another actor's movement onstage— anything from an actor entering the stage to one actor slapping another.

Curtain Call. At the end of a performance, the acknowledgment of applause by actors— the bows.

Dialogue. Words spoken onstage; usually involves more than one actor/character.

Director. Person carrying the ultimate responsibility for interpretation of script through control of actors and supporting production team.

Downstage (DS). The part of the stage closest to the audience.

Drama. The academic subject area into which theater falls.

Dress Rehearsal ("the Dress"). The final rehearsal before the performance. The actors are in costume and all technical problems should have been sorted out.

Ensemble. An acting group. Typically describes a group of performers who work well together, with no one actor outshining the others.

Entrance. 1) Place on a set through which the actor may appear. 2) Point in the script at which an actor appears onstage.

Exit. 1) The process of leaving the stage. 2) Point in the script at which an actor leaves the stage.

Fade. A fade is an increase, diminishment, or change in lighting or sound level.

Follow on Cue. A cue that is executed automatically after the previous one.

Hand Prop. Any prop handled by an actor.

Hit Your Mark. When an actor stands in the correct position (usually with regard to lighting), he or she is said to have "hit the mark."

House Lights. The decorative fixtures that light the auditorium while the audience is entering or leaving; usually they are dimmed or switched off during the performance.

Improvisation. When an actor who is "in character" makes up action or dialogue without prior scripting; often used in rehearsal or to cover other mistakes.

Intention. A single, temporary desire or goal that arises in a character within a scene.

Lighting Director. The individual in charge of working with the lighting crew to create a lighting design and run the lights during a performance.

Mime. Form of performance with no spoken words. Plot, character, etc., are conveyed to the audience by movement and gesture.

Monologue. A speech made by a single actor, usually in long paragraph form.

Motivation. The desires or goals of a character that propel him or her into action; the driving force of an inciting event that starts a story's progression.

Musical Director. The person in charge of the musical content of a show.

Notes. Following a rehearsal (or an early performance in a run), the director will give notes to the cast and crew about where to make changes, improvements, cuts, etc.

Objective. A single, temporary desire or goal that arises in a character within a scene. (Also called Intention.)

Offstage. Backstage area outside the performance area.

Open. To turn toward or face the audience.

Overture. The music that begins a performance.

Pace. The speed at which the story and action in a play runs.

Pantomime. Simply acting without words. This involves the use of the entire body, including facial expressions.

Part. An actor's part is his or her lines and directions; the whole performance of an individual.

Plot. The fundamental thread that runs through a story, providing the reason for the actions of the characters.

Preset. Used to describe any article or prop placed in its working area before the performance.

Principals (Primaries). The actors with lead or speaking roles in a show.

Projection. A request by a director for greater audibility from an actor. Not merely a matter of speaking louder, however; projection means to control volume, clarity, and distinctness so that the audience can better understand the lines being spoken.

Prompt. To feed an actor his next line when he has forgotten it. (Very unprofessional and a bad idea . . . but some people still do it!)

Pronunciation. Speaking clearly and precisely in order to be understood. It is important that the words being spoken can be heard clearly by everyone in the audience.

Props (short for "property"). Furnishings, set dressings, and all items large and small which cannot be classified as scenery, electronics, or wardrobe. Props handled by actors are called hand props, while props kept in an actor's costume are personal props.

Reader's Theater. Where the cast reads the play aloud with the script in hand, with or without gestures.

Rehearsal. The learning of the show by the cast and crew before a public performance.

Resolution. The point during a drama when the plotline reaches a conclusion and conflict is resolved.

Run-Through. A rehearsal at which all the elements of the production are put together in their correct sequence.

Scene. 1) A stage setting. 2) The blocks or parts into which a play is divided. 3) A particular setting of stage lighting that can be reproduced on demand.

Script. The text of the show, also containing information about settings, characters, costumes, etc., to aid the cast and crew.

Segue. Originally a musical term for an immediate follow-on; now used more generally for any immediate follow-on.

Set. All the scenery, furniture, and props used to create a particular scene.

Set Dressing. Props used to create atmosphere rather than having a function.

Sightlines. Lines indicating the limits of what an audience can see. The sightlines can be drawn on a plan or determined by someone in the auditorium.

Slapstick. Slightly manic but physical comedy that relies on often violent behavior to elicit laughter.

Stage Crew. Group of individuals who work behind the scenes setting props and scenery and handling the mechanical aspects of the production.

Stage Direction. In the script of a play, any instruction for the actors, or setting or character description.

Stage Left (SL). The left side of the stage as viewed by the cast facing the audience. Also Prompt Side, Camera Right.

Stage Right (SR). The right side of the stage as viewed by the cast facing the audience. Also Opposite Prompt, Camera Left.

Stage Set. All of the scenery in a scene. The stage set creates the physical setting—or sense of place—in which the action of a scene occurs.

Strike. To clear the stage of scenery and other materials, or to remove a specific article.

Supporting Cast. Actors who are not playing major parts.

Technical. The functions essential to a play other than those of the cast's actual interpretation of the script, particularly the set, lighting, etc.

Theme. The central idea of a play.

Typecast. When an actor or actress is cast repeatedly in the same kind of role or character. Happens with actors who have a distinctive look, voice, or stature.

Understudy. An actor who learns the part of another and is ready to step into their shoes, should they not be able to perform due to illness or some other reason.

Upstage. The part of the stage farthest from the audience.

Upstaging. Deliberately drawing focus onstage.

Walk-Through. Rehearsals at which the actors go through entrances, moves, and exits to make clear any changes or alterations that may be necessary.

Wardrobe. General name for the costume department, its staff, and the space they occupy.